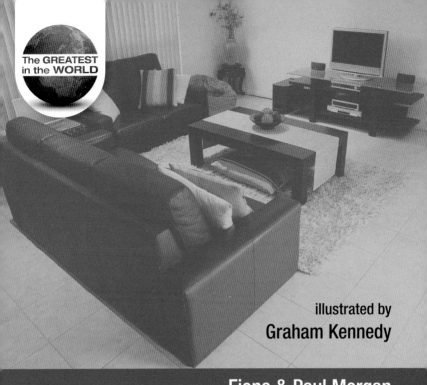

illustrated by
Graham Kennedy

Fiona & Paul Morgan

The Greatest
Property
Developing
Tips in the World

A 'The Greatest in the World' book

www.thegreatestintheworld.com

Illustrations:
Graham Kennedy
gkillus@aol.com

Cover & layout design:
the designcouch
www.designcouch.co.uk

Cover images:
© Marilyn Barbone; © Maxim Kulemza; © Kwest; © FrankU
all courtesy of www.fotolia.com

Copy editor:
Bronwyn Robertson
www.theartsva.com

Series creator/editor:
Steve Brookes

First published in 2006 by Public Eye Publications

This edition published in 2007 by
The Greatest in the World Ltd., PO Box 3182
Stratford-upon-Avon, Warwickshire CV37 7XW

Text and illustrations copyright © 2007 – The Greatest in the World Ltd.

A CIP catalogue record for this book is available from the British Library
ISBN 978-1-905151-69-1

Printed and bound in China by 1010 Printing International Ltd.

To Marjorie, Tony, Charlotte and Joss.

Contents

A few words from Fiona & Paul ...

We suspect that there's nothing unusual about our first introduction to the world of property development – we quite simply drifted into it! Having both experienced mixed fortunes in the past we really didn't know what we wanted to do. What we did know was that it had to be something we could do together and which had an element of creativity.

Fiona saw a small Victorian terraced house for sale about half a mile from our home. It was desperately in need of some T.L.C. having been tenanted for a number of years. We obviously knew the area well and were familiar with local demand. The asking price reflected its condition so we knew we could add value by carrying out a few essential improvements. A local independent adviser provided us with mortgage advice and within three months the house was ours. We did a substantial amount of the work ourselves and enjoyed every hair-raising, back-breaking minute of it! Six months later we were the proud owners of a small but very desirable house. We decided not to sell, but to rent and use the increased equity to finance our next purchase. By this time we realised that we were actually starting a business doing something we enjoy and (here's the good bit) – making a living!

Several years down the line we are still having just as much fun whilst progressing to slightly more ambitious projects. Currently we are converting an old disused chapel to three luxury apartments. At times this business can be nail-biting and frustrating, but never dull.

It has to be said that property development isn't for everyone, but what we have tried to do is give you a taste of what you can expect if you decide to give it a try. It should also help you decide whether you are the type of person who could be happy and successful in what is a relatively risky business.

We have learned so much over the years and, though this book is by no means an exhaustive guide, we hope that there's enough information here to help you make the right decision.

Good Luck!

Fiona & Paul

> Everyone says buying your first property makes you feel like an adult. What no one mentions is that selling it turns you right back into a child.

Anderson Cooper

Getting started

chapter 1
Getting started

Three words to forget

'Get rich quick'. This is NOT what property development is all about. However, by sticking to some basic principles you can build a satisfying and financially rewarding business.

Remember that in any property transaction we are dealing with large sums of money and therefore a businesslike attitude is crucial if you are to succeed. Here's a checklist to help keep your feet firmly on the ground.

1. Always be realistic about what you are trying to achieve, particularly in terms of finance, your own capabilities and your market.

2. Always provide for the unknown and unexpected. You should always have contingency plans both for additional funding and timing problems – for example, your electrician falls ill; can you replace him immediately so that your other contractors can continue as planned?

3. Get yourself organised. File all your paperwork, contracts and quotations where they can easily be found. Ensure that you keep proper accounts and retain all invoices and receipts.

4. Never be afraid to ask for advice. Talking to the right professional can save you both time and money.

Plan to succeed

Right from the start, decide what you want to achieve. Usually we are looking for the greatest profit in the least time. This means that you need to decide at a very early stage exactly what work you are going to do, who's going to do it, how long it will take and, just in case you forget, how much it will cost!

The search

Never underestimate the value of exhaustive research. Today we are fortunate enough to have the Internet at our disposal – probably the single most effective tool to assist us in the search for that ideal property. Estate agency websites are only the tip of the iceberg. The net will give you valuable up-to-the-minute information on prices, planning, development, transport and infrastructure, employment, leisure, education and more; in short, everything you need to locate those property 'hot-spots'. (See Contacts section for useful websites).

The search continues

.... and so it must! If you intend to make a living from property development the search should never stop. It's about making your investment work for you. If you are successful in your first venture and make a profit of say, £15,000, by all means give yourself a pat on the back. But unless that profit (or a substantial part of it) is reinvested in a new project it will soon dwindle. The sooner you crack on with project number two, three and so on the better. That's why the search is never over. As soon as you start work on one property, you should be actively looking for the next.

Red tape

These are just some of the aspects of officialdom that you might have to deal with. Overlooking or ignoring any of them could cost you dearly! Our advice is, if in doubt – ASK. In fact, it's a good idea to keep this list handy when considering any new project. Getting the answer you don't want too late in the day can completely ruin your plans. We'll be covering some of these in greater detail later.

- Planning permission.
- Listed buildings.
- Conservation areas.
- Building regulations.
- Fire regulations.
- Sound insulation.
- Party walls.
- Access and public highways.
- Car parking.
- Energy efficiency.
- Home Information Packs.
- Utility connection and supply.
- Neighbours' Rights.
- Tree Preservation.
- Flood Risk.

Types of development

Property development can take you in all sorts of directions. You might aim to start "small" and stay that way. That usually means one renovation or conversion at a time. You will gain valuable experience and knowledge, not least because renovations and conversions can turn out to be complex. When you start to strip down an older property you will often encounter unexpected problems. These could result in structural alterations that alter the appearance of the building for which you will need planning consent and, of course, building regulations approval.

During a recent conversion we encountered a disused well in the garden. It had not appeared in any plans and the vendors had no knowledge of it. After consultation with the building inspector it was agreed that the well be filled and capped for safety reasons.

In many ways, new build seems like a far simpler proposition; find a plot, design a house, obtain planning permission, build the house and sell it at a profit. If only it were that easy! The fact is that anything involving planning permission can take ages. Though eight weeks is the norm for most applications, there can be many hold-ups along the way. It can be an exciting process to see your ideas becoming reality, but you will need patience and determination in bucket-loads!

So far we have undertaken all three, renovation, conversion and new build. Each provides its own set of challenges, but if time and capital resources aren't plentiful, we would suggest that you begin by renovating a property or two just to get a feel for the business and find out if that is where your future lies.

In order to build a new house, you first need to find some land. On our crowded little island, space is at a premium and consequently land for building has become very expensive. Even in low-priced areas you might have to pay around £100,000 for a small plot and in a reasonably expensive area you might pay over £500,000 for a larger plot up to say 1 acre. As we mentioned earlier, this is where you might need a substantial amount of capital, since the high-street banks and conventional lenders will usually require a cash input from you of at least 25%.

There are specialist lenders who will lend much more but will charge a relatively high rate of interest because of the greater risk. They will make payment in stages and will allow the interest to accumulate until the loan is repaid from the sale proceeds. This is great for cash flow because it means that you don't have to worry about meeting monthly interest payments whilst running the project. You will need to factor that interest into your overall budget. A specialist lender will be able to help you prepare a cash flow forecast so that no one gets any nasty surprises along the way.

The employment of an architect will be a fairly substantial cost – perhaps up to £5,000 or more depending on the service you require. He will consult with both you and the planning authority, design the property or at least translate your ideas into detailed plans, prepare and submit your planning application, deal with any planning issues and 'red tape' such as Design & Access Statements and generally progress matters. If you want a hand with project management, many architects will also provide this service.

Some golden rules

Finance
Make sure it's in place. Much more on this later.

Chains
Where your property is involved in a series of transactions dependent upon each other. AVOID at all costs!

Survey
Unless you are a qualified surveyor or builder, this is an absolute must. Serious and costly structural defects often go undetected by the untrained eye.

Solicitor
Just like any other professional you encounter along the way, a good one is worth his/her weight in gold. Either use one you know personally or who is recommended. Keep in regular contact and ensure that he/she knows exactly what your business objectives are.

Accountant
Unless you are one, you'll need one! Taxation is ignored at your peril! Otherwise it's the same rule as 'Solicitor' above.

Contractors
You might feel competent to do some of the work yourself but you'll almost certainly need to use the services of professional tradesmen such as general builders, electricians, plumbers, carpenters, plasterers, roofers etc. Anyone can trawl the yellow pages, but that should be a last resort. Wherever possible use people you know or those who come recommended. If you have to venture into the unknown, request references and ask if you can view examples of their recent work. Regard with suspicion anyone who tries to fob you off or regards you as 'picky'.

Neighbours

Your project will almost always cause some degree of inconvenience to neighbours. However minor you consider this to be, put yourself in their shoes, especially when your property is a terraced house or flat and you'll be working in very close proximity. Think about the effects of noise, mess, dust, work on party walls and fences, skips outside the house, delivery of materials and parking of contractors' vehicles etc. We have always made a point of introducing ourselves to neighbours on day one. We explain what is about to take place, how long it's likely to take and ask permission for any access required. It's also a good idea to give a contact number so that they can reach you if they have any concerns about the work in progress. Taking this approach will not only help things go smoothly, but can be useful when things go wrong. One particularly windy evening we received a call from a neighbour telling us that some newly erected fencing had become dislodged and needed immediate attention to avoid serious damage.

Quick tip

HEART VS HEAD

We all have an idea of our 'dream home', but in this business it literally doesn't pay to get personal. Always remember it's a business; that means you must look for maximum return on your investment. For example, spending £10,000 on a state-of-the-art kitchen for a house aimed at the first-time buyer is madness. Always keep your target market in mind – it's their home you're creating, not yours.

" Don't stretch yourself too much with a mortgage. Buy within your means … it's not worth the sleepless nights. "

Sarah Beeny

The budget

chapter 2
The budget

This is probably the single most important aspect of any development project and therefore deserves maximum focus – so switch off the telly, take the 'phone off the hook and give this section your undivided attention! "Why?" you may ask. Well, given that your decision to develop property is based on a desire to make money, you won't be surprised to learn that, as in any successful business, there is a basic requirement to make a profit. Without profit, all your hard work, not to mention the risk involved, will be pointless.

The tips in this section are here to keep you on the straight and narrow. When you're knee-deep in estimates and your head is bursting with amazing designs for that cutting-edge kitchen or wow-factor wet-room, take a few moments to bring yourself back down to earth and remember why you decided to do this in the first place!

Get it right from the start

This is where it all begins. There is a maxim in this business that we cannot dispute, namely that the real money is made when you buy, not when you sell. If Tesco and Sainsbury are both selling identical potatoes at 50p per kilo and have paid 25p and 30p respectively to their suppliers, who has made the greatest profit? Obviously Tesco, not because their potatoes are superior but because they have been able to strike a better deal with their suppliers, i.e. when they bought.

Calculated risk

Property development is a risky business, but if you do as much as possible to ensure that all risks are calculated you will vastly increase your chances of success. The questions you should be asking at this stage are:

- Have I received and checked all my quotations?
- Have I agreed times and dates with all my suppliers/contractors?
- What is the likely timescale, including resale if this applies, of the whole project?
- Have I included an amount for contingencies?
- Have I sourced back-up tradesmen/suppliers 'just in case'?
- Is my finance in place?
- Have I prepared a cash flow forecast so that I know when payments are due and will be able to meet them as they arise?
- Have I covered all aspects of 'red tape'?
- Have I been totally honest and realistic in my answers to the above questions?

Where to look!

Here are some suggestions to consider which might help you find a bargain:

- Spring and autumn are peak times for the housing market. If you avoid these periods in your search you are more likely to strike a bargain.

- Ex-local authority properties are usually well built. They are good buys particularly if close to privately owned housing.

- Repossessions, though not quite the bargains they once were, can still be profitable. They are often in poor or neglected condition, but if structurally sound they can certainly do the business.

- Auctions can be a great way to secure that perfect property, but only if you know what you're doing – much more on this later.

So where do we start?

Let's assume you have researched your market and you are looking at a two-bedroomed Victorian terraced house in a popular residential area. You know from your research that it will appeal to first-time buyers, singles or young couples. You have looked at similar properties nearby and see that, in good condition, they have been selling for a maximum of £125,000.

Your property is on offer for £95,000 because it has been neglected over the years and needs a combination of repair and refurbishment to make it appeal to your target market. The difference between the purchase price of £95,000 and the likely sale price of £130,000 is £35,000 – your gross margin.

To start preparing your budget you must now quantify the following:

- Cost of labour and materials.
- Cost of finance.
- Legal fees.
- Estate agency fees.
- Surveyor's fees.

Once you have calculated these costs and subtracted them from your gross margin of £35,000, you will be left with your profit figure. Only then can you decide, based on your own circumstances and expectations, whether this is a worthwhile project. Generally, you should be looking at a figure of 20% as your gross profit after deduction of your renovation and other costs. Let's look at the figures using the example above:

Purchase price	£ 95,000
Legal/finance cost	£ 1,200
Estate Agency	£ 1,500
Survey fee	£ 500
Renovation	£ 9,000
Total cost	£107,200
Sale price	£130,000
Gross profit	£ 22,800 or 21.26%

This development satisfies the 20% rule in that the gross profit of £22,800 exceeds 20% of the total costs of £107,200. Depending on your circumstances, an element of taxation might apply – more on this later.

Time vs profit

"Procrastination is the enemy of profit." Never was a truer word spoken, especially when we're talking about property development. It's wise to remember that in the world of property there are many factors outside your control. Common sense tells us therefore that we should act promptly to minimise the chance of things going wrong. Some of the following tips might appear painfully obvious, but it's precisely because of their obvious nature that they are so often overlooked.

1. Is all necessary finance in place for both the purchase and the development? (Don't forget to include a contingency fund).

2. Once you have found your ideal property, check into the circumstances of your vendor. Is he/she purchasing another property? How soon can he/she complete? You need to identify as quickly and as accurately as possible the date on which you can commence work.

3. If you are employing professionals, keep in touch with them and ensure that they can start work in accordance with your schedule.

4. If you are sourcing materials, ensure availability and delivery both meet your requirements.

5. Are there any legal issues to address, e.g. The Party Walls Act in relation to terraced and semi-detached houses and flats? Remember, you cannot legally start work until the necessary notices have been served on your neighbours.

6. Is your development scheme likely to require planning consent or building regulations approval? These matters need to be checked out in the very early stages. If you ignore this your local planning authority could force you to stop work immediately or, worse still, you might have to undo work already done — more time, more money!

7. Check your work schedule thoroughly and if you are in any doubt, consult your professionals. For example, if the property requires damp-proofing and replastering as well as rewiring, who is booked to start work first, your electrician or your damp specialist? It's clearly better to have your rewiring done before any new plastering is carried out. Friction between your contractors on site can lead to expensive and frustrating delays.

8. Above all, stick to your plan! This section is all about the use of time and its effect on the profitability of your project. In most cases we all encounter the unexpected to some degree (hence the need for a contingency fund) but your potential biggest enemy is you! If you are not clear at the outset about what you want to achieve, your chances of success are immediately reduced. There is no greater waste of time, and therefore money, than constantly 'chopping and changing' things as you go along. Your budget and schedule will become distant memories, and with them the chance of making a worthwhile profit.

Keep it real

When preparing your first budget, accuracy is essential. 'Guesstimates' are fine once you have a few completed projects under your belt – in fact the ability to quickly assess the potential cost of a project is a skill you will acquire as you continue in the business. In the early stages, however, you will need to spend time collating figures for labour, materials, professional fees etc. so that you can be sure that the project is viable. After all, property is all about risk and reward, so you need to do all you can to minimise the risk.

Don't be afraid

Particularly when you are asking for estimates from professionals. Solicitors and surveyors are easy. They are required by law to provide full written quotation of their fees and disbursements and, unless the job becomes unexpectedly complex, this will be the figure you can count on. On the other hand, your local builder, plumber, electrician might come to look at the job and say something like "We're probably talking about something in the region of five, maybe six thousand all in".

Well, that's fine, but it poses more questions than it answers.

- Is it five, or is it six thousand?
- Is VAT included?
- Are all materials included?
- How long will the job take?
- When can you start?

To avoid problems later, you need to provide your contractor with a full specification of the work required. In turn, he needs to provide you with a full written quotation that answers all of the above questions. Never be afraid to ask for this.

It is very important to remember the difference between a quotation and an estimate. A quotation is a fixed price offer that can't be changed once accepted by the customer. This holds true even if the contractor has to carry out more work than was expected. An estimate, on the other hand, is an educated guess at what a job may cost but it isn't binding on the part of the contractor. The final costs could rise considerably depending on what other work or materials are found to be needed as the job progresses.

It pays to be picky!

(In moderation.) It's amazing what you can learn, and save, by researching, talking to, and negotiating with suppliers. Building contractors have often told us that because of time restraints, they are unable to obtain the best deals on materials. For obvious reasons, they will pay more in return for reliability and quality from a supplier. These costs are passed on to you. So, find out what your contractor is paying for materials he has agreed to include. It really does make sense for you to provide them if the cost is less and they can be delivered on time. Over the years we have bought central heating boilers, timber, fencing panels, laminate flooring and kitchen appliances all at lower prices than could be obtained by our contractors.

Use your contacts

Friends, family, work colleagues – they can all be great sources of useful information. Do you know someone who has recently employed a plumber to install a new bathroom? Were they impressed? Was the work of a high standard and competitively priced? Over time you will collect many useful names and 'phone numbers and gradually build your team of trusted professionals and suppliers.

Put it in writing

As mentioned earlier you need to obtain written quotations/ estimates for work required. However, particularly where you are employing a main contractor to bring in the various skills, you should wherever possible get a commitment to a written contract. Such a contract should specify:

- The work to be done.
- A schedule or timetable of work.
- The materials to be included where applicable.
- The overall timescale of the job.
- The total price for the job.
- The charge-rate for additional work arising.

Ironing out these details at the start will make for a very much smoother ride for all concerned.

NOTE: If you are tight for time, you might like to negotiate a performance bonus clause. Why not suggest to your contractor that you pay him a 10% bonus if the job is finished, say, seven days or more ahead of schedule? Conversely, you might like to consider a penalty clause whereby your contractor agrees to forego a percentage of his charge if he finishes late.

See Page 138 for an example of a simple building contract.

The more the merrier

Always try to get three quotations for each job. You'll be amazed at the range of prices quoted. We recently received quotes from three local builders giving figures of £3,900, £7,100 and £10,500 for the same work. In that particular case, the least expensive quote won the business not only because of his price. His firm had been recommended to us and, after making several 'phone calls we were able to establish that his work was of a very high standard.

We also made enquiries into the other two quotations. The builder who quoted £7,100 was regarded as 'good but a bit expensive' by two local people we spoke to. Finally, the last contractor who quoted £10,500 agreed, when pressed, that the job was a little too small for him – in other words, he didn't really want it.

A nice little earner

Well, it certainly can be if you get it right. But don't expect miracles! The function of a business at its lowest level is to earn you a living. If you are brave or fortunate enough to be able to go into property development full time without a regular income from elsewhere, then, long before you read this book you should have been asking yourself "how am I going to live for the next six months?". If that isn't the case, then you really do need all the help you can get!

Let's spell out the cold hard facts:

Example:

Purchase of sad, neglected house	£100,000
Mortgage available	£ 70,000
Deposit required	£ 30,000
Renovation and legal costs	£ 45,000
Projected sale price	£200,000

In short, if you were to go for this project, you would need access to:

£30,000 deposit

£20,000 – £40,000 renovation costs. (Some lenders will lend you 50% of the renovation cost).

£££££ – LIVING COSTS for at least the next six months!

Assuming you had the whole £75,000 to put into the project, you would turn this into a fund of £130,000 on completion of the sale – a pre-tax profit of £55,000 thank you very much!

BUT, if you need to work full time on the project and have no other income and you need £2,500 per month to live on, then you need at least six months' income (or £15,000) to survive! This would still leave you with £40,000, a very respectable return in this example.

The whole point of this is to remind you that you need to budget for your own living costs for the duration of any project. Not only will you get a much more realistic feel for the viability of each opportunity, but you'll also keep yourself out of financial trouble!

Know your limitations

When faced with a tight budget and a pile of builders' estimates with enough financial weight to flatten your project before you start, it's always tempting to have a go yourself to save money. "Just how difficult can it be to skim a ceiling ... put a new roof on ... remove that fireplace ... install that shower?" Imagine how much money you'll save, imagine how self-satisfied you'll feel because you did it!

Well, that might be so for some of us, but for most people it's a futile exercise. What money you save is lost purely in time – we are always slower than a good professional.

The professional's standard of work will almost always be better than ours, and of course, if everything isn't quite right, we have someone to complain to! Another slightly worrying aspect of this is that, if your own attempt at a particular job goes wrong, you will still have to employ a professional to put things right; more time – more money!

Your time is far better spent making sure the current project runs smoothly, on time and on budget. If you're serious about property development, you should already be searching furiously for the next property – time is money!

Can you do it?

A final checklist.

- Decide whether you are buying to sell or to let. They are vastly different propositions and you do need to decide the direction of your project at the outset.

- If you are thinking of buying to let, again do your research to ensure that the figures stack up and that your plans won't grind to a halt through lack of funds.

- Look at your own skills as objectively as possible and be prepared to pay professionals to do those jobs you cannot realistically tackle.

- Constantly check and re-check your budget so that it's as accurate as it can be. Don't forget to allow an extra 10% for those all-important contingencies.

- Be thorough in your initial assessment of the building; if you have any doubts about the fabric of the building, a structural survey is the only sensible option and could save you thousands of pounds.

- Don't fall into the common trap of poor finishing. When all the hard (and largely invisible) work is done, make sure that the final finish is beyond criticism. Only then will you have the best chance of realising a speedy sale at a top price.

"I told my mother-in-law that my house was her house, and she said, "Get the hell off my property."

Joan Rivers

Legal & financial

chapter 3
Legal & financial

The nature of this book is a little like the business itself, namely lots of important considerations tend to overlap. So from time to time you'll read something that you are convinced we've already written – and you might well be right! Although we believe that all of the tips we have included are vital to your success, some are so wide-ranging that they will necessarily appear, to re-enforce the point, in different sections of the book.

We can't stress enough the importance of getting these two aspects right. They are as much a part of the business as you are! Without the correct financial and legal foundations in place, your business is doomed. We sometimes tend to be cynical in our attitudes towards lawyers, accountants, bankers etc. but without their expertise and specialist knowledge our dreams would come to nothing.

Our experience has certainly proved this point. On one occasion our surveyor pointed out the remains of a chimney breast that was on the verge of collapse. The remedy was simple and inexpensive. Had this not been spotted, the damage to the property would have been very costly and could well have prevented its sale. On another occasion, it was the eagle-eye of our solicitor that alerted us to an old agricultural restriction that had not been registered. That could have been a very expensive mistake indeed!

Call in the experts

Here's a list of the most important ones; it's not exhaustive, but these are the people whose expertise is invaluable:

- Solicitor.
- Accountant.
- Independent financial adviser.
- Chartered surveyor.

Your solicitor will ensure that the property becomes yours without any nasty surprises, and will also help you dispose of it as smoothly and quickly as possible.

Your accountant will show you how to keep accurate records of all your business transactions and should make you substantial tax savings.

An independent financial adviser will steer you through the mortgage maze and find the best finance deal for you. Like any professional, he will charge you a fee, but if he's any good, he will save you that fee many times over through the quality of his advice.

The trained eye of a **chartered surveyor** can save you a fortune. The minimum you should pay is a Homebuyers Report before you commit to purchase. It will at least give you peace of mind or at best point out any structural defect that might need attention. Serious defects can include subsidence and dry rot. Having to rectify these could completely wreck your budget and therefore affect your decision to buy.

YOUR LOCAL PLANNING OFFICER

Most of the legal red tape should have been dealt with by your solicitor during the conveyancing process. However, when it comes to starting work, you need to bear in mind such things as planning permission, building regulations approval, the Party Walls Act, conservation areas, listed buildings etc. If in doubt, always ask before you start work. Mistakes can be time-consuming and costly.

More experts?

Being new to property development, you might by now be thinking "Surely, there can't be more!" However, as you become more involved and experienced, you will find that there is an enormous number of people whose knowledge and expertise you might be seeking. Never be afraid or embarrassed to ask for advice. Many experts will welcome your enquiries, not least because it shows that you are professional in your approach and clearly intent upon doing the job properly.

Your Local Planning Officer

He/she will appreciate clear and timely communication – it makes his/her job a lot easier. If your project is likely to involve planning issues, make an appointment to meet face-to-face at your local planning "surgery". Most local authorities usually hold these weekly and they are a great opportunity to learn and establish a rapport with your planning authority.

Building control

Each local authority employs a number of Building Control Officers or Inspectors. Contrary to popular belief, these are not people who take delight in closing down projects or insisting that new work is demolished because it contravenes Building Regulations. We have always found them helpful, supportive and happy to provide information. Their job largely involves keeping abreast of and interpreting a vast amount of government legislation in order to ensure that our work meets required safety and environmental standards.

Quantity surveyor

For larger projects, a quantity surveyor, as the name suggests, will be able to advise you independently on the amount, type and cost of materials you will require. In some cases your bank or finance company might require you to use a Q.S. to confirm these aspects of your budget and to report periodically on progress of the work.

Structural engineer

Particularly in the case of older property where defects might have been detected, a structural engineer will be able to advise you on remedial action. He/she will also be of help if you are considering major structural alterations.

Plan to succeed

One of the builders we regularly use, an ebullient Welshman, runs his business on the motto "Cash flow is King". He happens to be very successful and clearly lives by his motto. He's now so successful that he is trying to minimise his taxable income – clearly no cash flow problems for him!

Before you do anything else, make sure your finance is in place. Some lenders will ask you for a cash flow forecast along with a business plan. Their reasoning is that:

1. They naturally want to see that your proposition is viable, both for you and for them.

2. The project has a much greater chance of success if you have done plenty of preparation and can be as sure as possible that you aren't going to run out of money partway through the project.

If you've never done a business plan or a cash flow forecast before, have a word with your Accountant.

Who needs a contract?

The fact is we all do. If you're involving family, friends, private investors, anyone who will be investing money, time or resources in your project, you must draw up a contract that makes clear to everyone their rights, duties, obligations and rewards. Where family and friends are involved, most of us are naturally inclined to dispense with such formalities. This route can be a disaster in waiting. In short, don't think of a contract as being something that ties us all down, but rather as something that is designed to protect everyone.

Council tax

Fortunately there is total exemption where a property is unoccupied; however, this only applies for a six-month period. So, for example, if you buy a property that has been empty for say three months prior to completion of your purchase, then you have three months' exemption remaining. It follows therefore, that if a property has been unoccupied for more than six months when you buy, there might be a partial exemption, the amount of which will vary according to your local authority.

What if?

As in any speculative venture, you must ask yourself a number of questions before you commit to anything. What is more, you must be satisfied with your answers. Unless you can do this, you will be kidding yourself that success is just around the corner. Here are a few of the most common questions you should be asking:

- What if there are hidden defects in the property?
- What if the work takes longer than expected?
- What if additional costs are involved?
- What if it takes longer to sell than expected?
- What if I am let down by a builder, plumber, electrician etc?

Depending on your circumstances, there'll be more of these, but if one or more of your answers means problems, you must not be afraid to walk away. There will be other deals.

Raising the money

For most of us, this means borrowing the major part of the funds required by way of a mortgage. Many experienced property developers work on the basis that you should use as little of your own money as possible, which is generally a good philosophy to adopt. However, when you are new to the business, there's no escaping the fact that you will need some capital to get started. You might have savings, access to family capital, a maturing insurance policy or an existing loan or credit facility. Whatever is available, you must be willing to make a financial commitment at the outset.

If you really feel uneasy about the risks involved, or don't feel confident about your ability to manage large sums of money, then think very seriously about whether developing is the right business for you. If you just can't wait to get started, then the following list will give you an idea of what you will need.

Deposit for the purchase – at least 5% of the purchase price (don't bank on getting a 100% mortgage).

Survey fee – for peace of mind – set aside at least £500.00.

Legal fees – the amount will depend on a number of factors, but could be at least £1,500.00. Ask your solicitor for a quotation.

Stamp duty – only applies in relation to properties costing in excess of £120,000; (1% up to £250,000 and 3% in excess of £250,000).

Planning application fees – these will apply if your project requires Planning Permission. Assume up to £300.00 per dwelling.

Building regulations approval fees – these are almost certain to apply if you are carrying out a major renovation of an older property. Average fee is about £70.00.

Architect's fees – if you are engaging an Architect, obtain a detailed quotation. An Architect will normally require payment in stages as the job progresses.

Renovation cost – we can't stress too much how important it is to make this as accurate as possible. It represents by far the biggest slice of your total budget and your degree of success will be determined by your ability to get this right. With your first venture, it will seem an impossible task, so enlist some professional help at the outset. Further down the line, having completed a few more projects, you will have gained a huge insight into costing work and materials.

Contingency fund – this should be at least 10% of your renovation budget. Trust us – things can and will go wrong!

Other financing options

There will be other costs later, such as legal and estate agency fees relating to your sale. Although these need to be included in your overall budget, you won't need to fund these up front, since they will be paid from your sale proceeds.

If you have funds available for these essential items, you can seriously think about getting started. If you don't, and you are still keen to go ahead, you might consider other options to help raise finance.

Remortgaging your home

You might have an amount of available equity here, so in the first instance you should talk to your mortgage lender, who could help with a further advance (i.e. an increase in your current mortgage); you might be able to obtain a better deal by taking your mortgage to another lender. Since the mortgage market is now very sophisticated with literally hundreds of options available, our advice is to consult an independent advisor who specialises in mortgages. As always, be sensible about what you can afford.

A business partnership

There's nothing new about this, but it really can work with property development. Quite simply, most businesses require two things in order to start trading – capital and expertise. You might have all the necessary skills to be a successful developer, but, guess what – no money!

You might know someone who has money but none of those skills. By working as a partnership you can both benefit by building a business. A good way to test the water is to agree with your potential partner that you will work together on one project, each providing the appropriate resources. For instance, your partner takes care of all financial, legal and accounting functions leaving you to concentrate on the task of project managing the job from start to finish. You agree on a profit share at the outset and enter into a legally binding contract. If you are successful, you'll want to repeat the exercise, or perhaps one or both of you will decide it's not for you. Either way you will have gained some valuable experience.

Development finance

This is made available by specialist lenders. Unlike bank or building society products, this finance is tailored specifically to the needs of the developer. As such, it is more flexible, has a higher risk profile and is therefore much more expensive.

Typically such a lender will advance up to 75% of the value of the property in its current state, more in some cases, together with up to 100% of the cost of the development work, the latter being advanced in stage payments as the work progresses.

One of the most appealing and useful features of this type of finance is that interest can be 'rolled up' until resale of the development.

If you think the above would apply to your particular plans, try contacting a few via the Internet – just type in 'development finance' and your search engine will do the rest. Alternatively, your financial adviser might have some contacts in the field.

Family and friends

We prefer to call them private investors. If you have explored all other avenues and still have a shortfall, you might wish to consider giving others the opportunity to literally invest in your project. Bearing in mind that you are effectively asking people to participate in a business venture, you must be prepared to offer them a realistic but attractive return that reflects the risk involved. If a friend or a member of your family is prepared to put up £5,000.00 to cover your shortfall, you could offer to repay say £6,000.00 on completion of the sale. If the whole project takes six months, you have given your investor a massive 20% return on his or her stake – equivalent to 40% per annum!

This is obviously expensive borrowing and should only be undertaken if all else fails, but it can often mean the difference between success and failure in the early stages.

A word of caution here; never enter into such an agreement without agreeing terms in full and having a legally binding contract drawn up by a solicitor. You should insist that your investor takes independent legal advice before committing.

DID YOU KNOW ... ?

Interest on ALL borrowing used to finance your project, no matter what the source, can be offset against profit for tax purposes. So, if you've borrowed on credit cards or from family/friends, remember to keep accurate records of what this has cost.

> The universe is merely a fleeting idea in God's mind – a pretty uncomfortable thought, particularly if you've just made a down payment on a house.

Woody Allen

Auctions

chapter 4
Auctions

This section, in many ways, closely relates to the previous one simply because it's one area where you need to be fully aware of both the legal and financial implications before you even set foot in an auction room. However we have given auctions their own section in view of the many different rules that apply.

The atmosphere at auction can be exciting, especially when the bidding is fast and furious. When you have done all your research and are convinced that you have found THE property, it is easy to get carried away. It's vital, therefore, that you keep a clear head and stick to your original maximum figure, otherwise you could be throwing away your profit at the fall of the hammer! When a bid is accepted at auction, this is the equivalent of exchange of contracts in the normal conveyancing process; the result is that you are contractually bound to complete the purchase. The benefit here is that the process is much quicker and, if your bid is successful, you'll be able to complete and start work in a very short space of time – so enhancing your chance of making a good profit.

Before we get to the auction itself, it's necessary to understand why vendors use auctions as a means of sale. There are many reasons, and being aware of them will be of enormous help to you in evaluating the potential of a particular property, so let's ask the question …

Why are properties sold at auction?

There are several reasons why vendors will auction a property rather than put it on the open market in the conventional way. These reasons should always be borne in mind when your potential target property is being sold at auction:

1. **Out of the ordinary**
   It might be unusual in structure, appearance, location, layout etc. and therefore very difficult to value. This will result in an estate agent advising his client to go to auction as a means of letting the market decide what it's worth. Agent and client will usually agree privately on a 'reserve' price, the minimum figure for which the vendor will agree to sell. If that figure is not reached during the bidding on auction day, the property is withdrawn from sale.

2. **Structural faults**
   The property might suffer from some serious structural defect which would make it difficult to value for the open market. If the vendor has neither the means nor inclination to carry out the repairs, then he/she might feel that the quickest and easiest route to disposal is a sale by auction.

3. **Executor's sale**
   Where the owner of a property has died, the executors may either be under an obligation imposed by the owner's will to sell at auction, or it might have been the executors' decision to do so in order that all the beneficiaries are satisfied that the best possible price has been obtained.

4. **Repossession**
   Properties that have been repossessed by mortgage lenders are often sold at auction. Again, the mortgage lender has a legal obligation to the borrower to achieve the best price reasonably obtainable.

5. **The last resort**
   For some vendors, going to auction is a desperate measure. Perhaps they have tried to sell for long periods using several agents without success.

Particularly in numbers 1, 3, 4 and 5, the fact that the property is being auctioned is not necessarily a cause for alarm. It just means that the vendor's circumstances and attitude are such that auction seems the best way forward.

If you, as a property developer, have the time and resources to carry out repairs and turn a wreck of a house into a desirable home, then you are the ideal purchaser, PROVIDED that you have done your sums, asked all the 'what if' questions and are satisfied that this is a deal that will make you money.

Location

The very fact that a property is being auctioned might mean that all is not as it seems. Some things are more obvious than others. Close proximity to a rubbish tip, a sewerage plant, a pig farm, a large industrial site, a busy pub and difficult neighbours have all been reasons for a sale being hard to achieve. So, make sure you are satisfied as to location before taking things further.

Planning

This is another area that needs careful research. There might be planning applications currently being considered involving undesirable elements such as road widening schemes or large commercial building projects. Who wants to be overlooked by an office block or a factory unit?

Vendors' solicitors should provide what is often called a 'Legal Pack' when you first register your interest. This pack should contain, amongst other things, an up-to-date local search and plan. If there are any planning proposals that might affect the property, then they will be disclosed in the search results. If in doubt, consult your solicitor and/or the local planning office for clarification.

Condition

Unless you are buying a brand new property, NEVER purchase without a survey, or at least a Homebuyers Report; this is crucial when buying at auction. As we have said, there are all sorts of reasons why vendors go to auction, and one of them is that the property might otherwise be difficult to sell because of its condition. Unless you are an expert, you MUST have the building surveyed. Yes, it will cost you – but it could save you thousands of pounds, particularly if there is evidence of dry rot or subsidence. Such problems won't necessarily kill a deal, but if you are aware of them prior to auction, you will be able to assess the cost of remedial work and build this into your budget.

The 'invisibles'

The reasons for vendors going to auction are often obvious. Occasionally you will come across what appears to be a bargain because, having had your survey done and carried out all your checks, all seems well. But there could be reasons for the sale that are not on public record, e.g. troublesome neighbours, poor air quality due to nearby industry, a pub or club with a dodgy reputation, or constant heavy traffic. Spend some time in the area at different times of the day. Talk to local people and try finding out what it's like to actually live there.

Don't forget your cheque book!

If you bid successfully you will be required to sign a contract immediately and pay a deposit (usually 10% of the purchase price). In addition, the contract will stipulate a completion date upon which you will pay the balance of the purchase price and the property then becomes yours. You must have all your finance in place if you intend to bid.

Go to at least one auction as an observer before bidding to gain experience, and check with local estate agents beforehand to find out what similar properties in the area have fetched.

The guide price

Otherwise known as the bait, the 'Guide Price' is usually
anything but! Soon, you will realise that the property with
the guide price of say £150,000 eventually sells for £200,000
and, even more infuriating, the vendor had put on a reserve
price of £175,000! So, in most cases, ignore the dreaded guide
price – expect to pay considerably more.

Quick tip

GET USED TO IT

As we have said, the atmosphere at auction can be highly
charged. The best way to prepare yourself is to attend
one or two purely as an observer. It will cost you nothing
and is a great way to see and understand exactly what is
involved. By the time you are ready to bid seriously for a
property, the mystery and fear that often goes with it will
have disappeared. You can find out about forthcoming
auction dates from your local press, agents or the Internet.

Don't get carried away!

An auction can be a very exciting event, particularly if there's
a property you want to buy, so it's extremely easy to get carried
away by the adrenalin-charged atmosphere. Remember, you
have spent valuable time and money on your research, you
have prepared your budget and, most important of all, you have
established your maximum bid. If you exceed that figure, your
project starts to become less profitable. So, stay calm and stick
to your maximum figure – to do otherwise could be a disaster.

> **People are living longer than ever before, a phenomenon undoubtedly made necessary by the 30-year mortgage.**

Doug Larson

Know your market

chapter 5
Know your market

Whatever you are selling, success depends on knowing your customer. If you don't know what your customer wants you have little or no chance of making a sale. That's why you need to research your market thoroughly before embarking on any project.

Purchasers come in all shapes and sizes – single, married, sharing, families with children, couples planning children, single parent families, young, middle-aged, retired people. If you have bought a bungalow in an area surrounded by similar properties occupied by retired people, don't go for the "chic urban apartment" look favoured by young professionals.

The trick in this business is to find a property in an area where there is a healthy mix of all types and then ensure that it has the widest appeal. It's always tempting to put your own individual mark on a property at the design stage, but in doing so you can instantly alienate potential purchasers.

Likewise it's very easy let your own personal aspirations take over. We recently looked at a property that had been let. Prior to letting the vendor had renovated the house and had installed a very expensive range cooker. The tenants were students and the cooker required cleaning by professionals before the property was marketed!

Let's look at some simple but often overlooked rules for getting to know your market.

The population

Who lives there currently? Families, singles, retired people, young professionals? You need to know so that your property will appeal to the widest possible market. For example, a street where 90% of properties are rented to students is not likely to appeal to a couple with two young children, even if you have created their dream three-bed semi.

The area

What are the prospects for the future? Find out what's going on from the local council and the local press. Is it classified as a regeneration area? Are there any new or proposed road or rail schemes afoot? Are the big names from the High Street moving in? Big business is one of the best indicators of future growth and popularity. Conversely, if you find that there are lots of empty commercial premises around and there is a general atmosphere of degeneration, you will do best to move on and research another locality.

A good example from our own experience is an area of South Wales known as "The Valleys". Over the years, the area had fallen into decline as a result of mine and steelworks closures. However, in recent times the area has been the subject of several regeneration schemes including new road and rail links with major centres such as Cardiff and Newport. Many businesses have relocated there and the housing stock is expanding through new build schemes by major developers. Consequently the housing market received a much-needed boost over the past couple of years, making this a great area for the budding property developer.

WHAT THE PEOPLE WANT

Again ensure that there are local amenities such as shops, public transport, schools, entertainment etc. to satisfy the needs of your target market.

The right stuff

So, you have now identified the type of purchaser who will readily buy in your location. You must then ask "How can I make this property appeal to them?" For instance, young professionals, singles and couples tend to prefer the flexible living space offered by open-plan design where kitchen, dining area and lounge are effectively one room with three distinct functional areas. Experience also shows that the clean, uncluttered lines of modern kitchens and bathrooms also appeal, as does the presence of a shower in addition to, rather than instead of, a bath. Always remember, this is NOT YOUR HOME.

Nice house, shame about the garden

Often neglected or overlooked, the garden or 'outside living space' is something you should not ignore. It can make the difference between an average sale price and a top sale price or, at worst, the difference between selling and not selling. As before, your market must always be uppermost in your mind at the planning stage. If your purchasers are likely to have young children you should provide a safe play area, ideally a lawn. Any ornamental trees, shrubs etc should be positioned away from or at least bordering the lawn to ensure maximum chance of survival. Maintenance is also a key point. Working parents of young children don't usually have an awful lot of time for serious gardening, whilst young singles and professionals tend to regard the garden as an area for entertaining or relaxing. In both cases, go for a low maintenance approach using pots, planters, paved areas, gravel and, of course, a patio.

Period features

If your project involves an older property, it might include features such as cornices, ornate plasterwork, panelled doors, fireplaces, stained glass windows etc. that are typical of the period in which the house was built. As a general rule, these features should be retained wherever possible, since they are usually part of the reason why people are attracted to such properties. Windows are a particularly important issue. Your property might not be a listed building, but if it is in a conservation area don't even think about installing UPVC windows. Look around at neighbouring properties and get a feel for what other owners have done, and don't be tempted to tear the soul out of your house just because everyone else seems to have done so; after all, you want your property to stand out as being the 'must have' in that particular area.

Bathrooms & bedrooms; how far do we go?

No matter how long you've been property developing, this is a question that pops up on a regular basis, particularly when renovating older houses.

Victorian terraces, as we know, were not built with bathrooms. From the 1930's onwards, the bathroom became a standard feature in the new wave of house building, e.g. the classic 3-bedroom semi. By the 1950's many families living in older terraced properties felt that a bathroom was a basic amenity that should be available to everyone. The governments of the day, ever more conscious of the need to address issues of public health and hygiene, supported this view and made grants available to householders for the provision of bathroom and toilet facilities. In most cases, due to restrictions of cost and space, the new bathroom/W.C. appeared as a single storey extension at the back of the house. Since that time, things have moved on considerably, with new properties frequently providing multiple bath/shower rooms, en-suites and W.C.s.

The key to getting this right is to be aware of a buyer's expectations in your market. If your property has 3 bedrooms, a downstairs bathroom and is likely to appeal to a family with children, you would be seriously compromising your project by 'losing' a bedroom to provide an upstairs bathroom. On the other hand, if the main bedroom is of sufficient size, you could add value by installing an en-suite shower room and W.C. As usual, you must look at your potential market carefully and do the appropriate 'sums', bearing in mind that brand new plumbing upstairs could be expensive.

It's tangible, it's solid, it's beautiful, it's artistic. I just love real estate.

Donald Trump

The selling process

chapter 6
The selling process

This is the bit you've been looking forward to. It's the time when you finally get to find out whether all your hard work, doubts, fears, not to mention financial risks, have paid off. It's not surprising if you now approach this phase with some trepidation! However, as with all aspects of property development, it's best approached with a clear picture of what you want to achieve and a carefully drawn plan as to how you will succeed.

As we've said many times before, time is money, and you don't have to be actually spending money to lose it. If you've worked hard on your renovation, stuck to your schedule and finished on time and on budget, it is completely pointless to relax and wait for a sale to materialize. You must do everything possible to ensure that the right purchaser is found without delay.

If you fail to keep your eye on this ball, all sorts of problems could emerge, for example; interest is piling up on your borrowing and eating into your profit; spring has gone, everyone is away on holiday and your market is dead; you are committed to the maintenance and security of your empty property; prospective purchasers are suspicious because that "FOR SALE" board has been there for a long time; you've seen the next perfect project but your hands are tied because you haven't yet been able to release your capital. Let's be positive and look at a number of tips to help you through the process.

Estate agents

Engaging the services of a good agent can pay dividends. Pay as much attention to choosing an agent as you would to employing any other professional adviser. First select three local agents and invite them to carry out a valuation or market appraisal. From your research you should already have a fairly reasonable idea of your property's value and saleability. Don't be flattered by the agent who puts an unexpectedly high value on your property, particularly if the figure quoted is substantially different from those given by other agents. It is always best to take all three valuation figures, add them together and divide by three to calculate the average valuation. Bear in mind that most potential buyers will want to haggle, so be prepared for this when fixing your initial asking price.

Going it alone

In other words, selling privately without using an agent. Frankly, not recommended. You will save on fees, but your agent is far more likely than you to have the time, expertise and resources to achieve a profitable sale. In our experience a reputable estate agent, as with any other professional, will more than cover his/her fee by obtaining a better price than you could achieve yourself. If you were to consider the amount of time and expense involved in preparing your own marketing material, advertising, taking phone calls, conducting viewings and validating offers, you would not hesitate to employ an agent. If you want to continue developing, you'll need to make the best use of your time by seeking out the next project. Time spent on that aspect is the single most important part of your job as a developer if you are serious about a successful business.

Agent's strategy

Discuss each agent's sale strategy and capability. Do they use the Internet? Will they conduct all viewings on your behalf? What do you think of their advertising? Do they have a healthy mailing list of people looking for your type of property? If you are impressed by the number of their 'For Sale' boards seen locally, ask why there are so many and perhaps why so few 'Sold' signs. In the end, if the agent can be considered reputable, you need to feel that you can work with this person and that he or she will do everything possible to achieve the quickest sale at the best price. Once you are satisfied, you can then sign a formal agreement which should be for no longer than the minimum period.

Avoid multiple agency agreements wherever possible. Using two or more agents to market your property simultaneously should be a last resort. Apart from being expensive, it can send out the wrong signals to potential buyers, such as an unrealistically high price or that the property is, for some reason, undesirable.

Remember, if you have decided that you are going to continue developing in one geographical area, establish a working relationship with your chosen agent. This way you might be able to negotiate a discount on fees (repeat business is always appealing), and be alerted to future suitable properties as they come on the market.

Finally, a word on the fees. These do vary considerably, but remember that an extra 0.5% or 1.00% is insignificant if your agent achieves the right result.

Sales particulars

Don't be afraid to be critical here. Apart from accuracy (a legal requirement), the agents details will be, for many people, the all-important 'first impression' of your property. Consequently, they must present your property in the best possible light. Exterior photographs should be taken in good weather where possible and interior shots should include those areas considered to have the 'wow factor'. If the property benefits from an attractive garden or views, make sure that shots of these are included. Draft particulars will be submitted to you for approval, so this is your chance to ensure that you are making the most of the service.

In some cases an agent might suggest some additional marketing material, such as a brochure or a 'feature' advertisement in the local press. A brochure will obviously involve extra cost, but 'feature' advertisements can often be arranged at no extra cost if the agent is a regular advertiser. These are usually larger, stand-alone ads which will emphasise a particular aspect of your property to arouse maximum interest. Sometimes these are known as "Editorials" because although they appear amongst the agency ads, they resemble articles and almost never state the asking price. If potential buyers are sufficiently 'hooked' by the editorial, they will either phone the agent or refer directly to the main ad to ascertain the price.

We found our own house in just such an ad. The agent later told us that the property had been advertised conventionally for the previous two weeks without generating any interest whatsoever. As soon as the editorial was published, we found ourselves amongst many others who wanted to view.

On the market

So you are now officially on the market. Always allow your agent to conduct viewings, and obviously ensure that the property always looks its best. Buyers will feel far more relaxed during a viewing conducted by an agent rather than by the vendor. If you're not living there, check it after each viewing to ensure there are no muddy footprints left behind. If that's impractical, ask your agent to check on your behalf.

Another increasingly common marketing tool is the 'open day' where interested parties are invited to view the property at any time during a particular day. This often brings out the competitive streak in potential buyers and, if your property is well presented and the day is handled professionally, the result could be several offers, putting you firmly in the driving seat.

To make the best use of everyone's time, arrange with your agent a weekly telephone appointment to discuss progress, feedback from viewings etc. This will avoid pointless phone calls and messages. Ensure that you respond to any enquiries promptly and professionally. If you are dissatisfied with the agent's service, make it clear and state your reasons. Similarly, listen carefully to any advice the agent might give and consider it objectively before making any decisions.

Keep an open mind and be willing to make changes to your marketing strategy. If your property is 'sticking', analyse the feedback from viewers to find out why. It might be something as simple as an ambitious price tag. Whilst dropping the price is never a favourite option, you could authorise your agent to offer a discount if an interested party can complete within say six weeks, or perhaps give a 'stamp duty paid' incentive.

An offer is received

This should be relayed to you by your agent immediately it is made. Don't be tempted to accept the first offer, even if it meets your realistic expectations. The buyer's circumstances must be checked out thoroughly before you accept. Some questions you should be asking are:

Does the buyer have a property to sell and, if so, what stage has that sale reached? Even a realistic offer can turn out to be bad news if your buyer is involved in a chain of dependent sales and purchases.

Has the buyer organised his or her finance? Most lenders in today's market can issue an 'in principle' mortgage offer, showing that the applicant's request for a certain amount of money has been successful, subject only to a satisfactory valuation of the property. Not only does this save everyone's time, but it will also leave you confident of a quick sale to a buyer who is good for the money.

If the offer amounts to less than your asking price, ask why. Is it because the buyer is merely looking for a good deal, or perhaps there are certain matters that he or she feels adversely affect the value of the property? If there are criticisms about minor matters e.g. badly fitting doors, poor paint finishes etc. you might suggest fixing them in return for the full asking price or at least something nearer. If your suggestion is rejected, then you know that the buyer is after a better deal. At this point you might wish to consider the 'quality' of your buyer. Nothing to sell and finance organised means that this is your ideal buyer, and for that reason accepting a lower offer might be your best option.

Valuation

If any defects are revealed at this stage your options are fairly straightforward:

1. Reduce your price to allow for the cost of any remedial work.

2. Offer to repair the defect, and, if this is accepted, continue with the sale at the agreed price.

3. Occasionally, a defect will be found which requires a specialist report, e.g. timber and damp-proofing specialist or structural engineer. It is always wise to obtain such reports as there might be serious faults that could jeopardise a sale.

Completion

You (or your agent) have handed over the keys and your sale proceeds are winging their way into your bank account. Time for a celebration, and, if you are anything like us, almost time to start work on the next project. Remember, if you are going to be successful in this business, you must keep the momentum going. By the time you complete one sale you should be almost ready to complete on your next purchase. Immediately investing a proportion of your profit in the next project will ensure that your money is working hard for you. Whilst you look for the next property over the coming weeks or months, money sitting in your bank account has a habit of disappearing – fast!!

Scotland and Ireland:
Property law in both Scotland and Ireland is somewhat different from English law. If you are considering buying or selling in either, the following lists should help you.

Scotland

The job of an estate agent is done by a solicitor in Scotland. You should obtain a fee quotation which will include charges for both the sales and conveyancing processes. You are free to use an independent estate agent who will usually deal direct with your solicitor.

When your property is advertised for sale, the price will be described as 'Offers in excess of ....'. In Scotland, that means exactly what it says; the price shown is the minimum you will accept. Before making a formal offer, any interested party is obliged to have a survey carried out.

Where you have several interested parties, you will announce a closing date and time for receipt of written offers, at which point you must make a decision as to which offer you will accept. You are not bound to accept the highest offer, or indeed any of them if you don't wish to do so.

The next stage of the process is regarded as having the advantage over the English system. Once an offer is accepted, your solicitor and the purchaser's solicitor will exchange letters (known as 'missives') confirming the terms of sale. This only takes a day or two and is legally binding on both parties. As a result, the dreaded practice of gazumping we experience in England is totally excluded.

Once all the terms contained in the missives have been satisfied your solicitor will arrange completion, send the title deeds to the purchaser's solicitor, repay any outstanding mortgage in the usual way and account to you with the sale proceeds. (Champagne time!).

For more helpful information on the Scottish system, please see the Useful Contacts section at the end of the book.

Ireland

As in England, most property is sold privately using an estate agent. Choose an agent who is a member of the Irish Auctioneers & Valuers Institute.

Your property will be advertised and offers invited. If there is a lot of interest, your agent might suggest a 'sealed bid' strategy, whereby offers are to be submitted in writing by a certain date and time. As in Scottish and English law, you are not obliged to accept any offer.

On acceptance of offer a 5% deposit is normally required, in return for which the property is taken off the market. This doesn't mean that other offers cannot be entertained prior to exchange of contracts – so gazumping hasn't yet been eradicated in Ireland.

Estate agents in Ireland are also, for the most part, auctioneers. Consequently, selling a property by auction is far more common in Ireland than elsewhere. Auction rules are the same as in England. (See Section 4 for a full guide to auctions).

No man feels more
of a man in the world
then when he has
a bit of ground that
he can call his own.
However small it is
on the surface, it is
four thousand miles
deep; and that is
a handsome property.

Charles Dudley Warner

Selling the dream

chapter 7
Selling the dream

In Chapter 5 you learned how to identify your target market. In this section we're going to look at a few simple ways to enhance the perception of the lifestyle or 'dream' you are offering. The key word here is 'perception'.

Prospective purchasers will usually have a fairly clear idea of what kind of home they would like to buy. It's usually related to comfort, practicality, lifestyle and a general feeling of happiness and well-being. As a developer, your job is to meet these aspirations as far as possible whilst making a profit and building a successful business. You will always have both financial and practical restraints, so you will need to be aware of steps you can take to maximize the appeal of your property without 'breaking the bank'.

If you are employing reputable tradesmen the finish should be something you are completely satisfied with. Likewise, if you have done some of the work yourself you should be able to stand back and honestly admire the results. If this isn't the case, then you are heading for trouble. Whether it's decoration, joinery, tiling, plumbing or electrical work, it all has to be done to a high standard. If the finish is not good, it will raise suspicions about what lies beneath and either slow down the sale process or destroy it completely.

The purpose of these tips is to enhance the good work that has already been done. None will conceal a shoddy finish.

Furniture

Use very sparingly. Certainly don't go out and buy a load of new pieces to 'dress' your property. This will reduce your profit and leave you with items you won't need again, since it's highly likely that they will be totally unsuitable for your next project. There are however occasions when you will need to define a particular space to show how it can best be used.

For instance, you might want to demonstrate that a small bedroom is suitable for use as a guest room and will accommodate a double bed. In just such a case we bought a second-hand divan bed for £15.00 and covered it with clean white linen – an instant guest room!

Optical illusion

Not as complicated as it sounds. Narrow hallways and passages can be instantly enlarged by the strategic hanging of a mirror to create the illusion of space. Mirrors are also useful for making the best of limited light sources, thus making any room seem bigger and brighter.

Wherever possible, try to demonstrate the purpose of a particular space. For instance, if you have an open plan design with a dining area, a table and chairs will clearly show how the space can be used. You don't necessarily need to set the table for dining – a vase of flowers, indoor plant will do very nicely. Remember: no clutter – less is more.

Distraction

Not all properties enjoy stunning views over picturesque countryside. If the view from part of your property is less than inspiring, you should consider putting up a plain blind – much cheaper than curtains and can be used again elsewhere.

More distraction

Another method to divert the viewer's eye from the less-than-stunning view is to hang a painting. This will create a focal point for the room and might just distract your viewer from looking out of the window!

Clean and tidy

You might think this is so obvious it doesn't need mentioning. However, on our researching travels we have been amazed at the number of vendors who have clearly spent time and money on their properties only to ruin the effect by, for example:

- Leaving a skip on the drive or road directly outside the property.
- Leaving tools and building materials lying around the house.
- Failing to pick up junk mail, free newspapers etc. from behind the front door.
- Forgetting to clean windows.
- Failing to ensure that the kitchen and bathroom are spotlessly clean.
- Failing to keep the garden tidy and mow the lawn.

Accents

No, you don't need to learn a new way of speaking – these are merely items that might make your house look more like a home and enhance the general feel of the place. Try not to go overboard with these because less is definitely more. They should complement or contrast your décor and generally give the impression that some care has been taken in providing the finished product. Here is a list of items you might wish to use:

- A bottle of wine (and perhaps 2 glasses).
- 2 coffee mugs, a cafetière.
- A bowl of fruit.
- Fresh flowers (must be tended and changed regularly).
- Pot plants (don't forget to water them).
- A bottle of olive oil.
- Towels and soap to 'soften' the bathroom.
- Cushions (on the bed or sofa, assuming these are present).
- Candles.
- Logs in a fireplace.

There are many more, but we have used all of the above to good effect – SPARINGLY!

Stay interested

Now we know that after several months of hard graft, the odd sleepless night and a chunk of stress thrown in for good measure, we feel immense relief when the property is finally ready for marketing. Occasionally we might feel as if we have lost all interest in the project – this is all perfectly natural. But if we are going to achieve what we set out to do, i.e. make the greatest profit in the least amount of time, then we cannot afford to sit back just yet. Even if we have lost interest, we simply cannot afford to let anyone else know. Your property needs to look its best AT ALL TIMES if you are expecting someone to think seriously about buying it. After all, how can you expect anyone to take an interest in something you no longer care about?

- If you've used fresh flowers, go back and change them regularly.

- Mow the lawn; keep the weeds under control.

- Make sure the windows and exterior paintwork are kept clean.

- If it's winter time and the weather is cold. Make sure you keep the place aired with some background heating. Cold houses are extremely uninviting.

- Again, especially in winter, viewers visiting after work will be in darkness, so make sure all lights are in working order.

- Remove junk mail and newspapers regularly.

- Clean and protect all carpets and floor coverings from muddy shoes.

- Make sure neighbours have got your 'phone number in case of emergency, e.g storm damage.

So, don't ever forget these finishing touches – for very little time, money and energy they will make an enormous difference when it's time to sell.

Ten top tips for budget savings

Finally in this section we're going to look at ten simple ways to help keep your budget under control and maximise your profit:

1. Kitchens with a wow-factor can be expensive. Try looking at flat-pack carcasses for the main body of the kitchen, then you can afford to create that wow-factor using granite worktops, state-of-the-art taps, fittings and stylish door/drawer handles.

2. If a bathroom suite is in good condition and it's white, think carefully before condemning it to the skip. With a good clean and some new stylish taps, it will do the job just as well as a new one.

3. In period properties, it's not only cheaper but far more desirable to retain period features wherever possible. This will save you time, money and help you get the best possible price.

4. If you decide to dress your property for the market, see which items you can borrow from home, friends or family before heading for the shops. Again this will save you both time and money.

5. Shop around for suppliers. Don't assume that your builder, plumber, electrician etc. can always get a better price than you. It's simply not true. Doing business on the Internet can be a great way to make savings here.

6. Keep a watchful eye on the calendar. Time is money. The quicker the turnaround, the greater the profit. If, having worked out the figures, you feel that it's worthwhile, talk to your contractor about a performance bonus. Considerable savings can be made just by getting the job finished sooner.

On the other hand, a penalty clause in the event of a late finish can also be very useful in safeguarding your cash.

7. There are certain unskilled jobs that anyone can do, so, if you have the time, the inclination and you're fit enough, by all means muck in with your builder and go for it! Jobs such as stripping out unwanted fixtures and fittings, hacking off plaster, generally clearing the site, tidying the garden and general labouring all cost money if someone else has to do them. As well as being able to keep an eye on things, you're also bound to learn a lot.

8. Friends and family can be a great source of help. They can often contribute skills, knowledge and labour (see 7 above). However, be careful not to take advantage and always do or give something to show your appreciation – remember you are benefiting from their time and expertise. Forget this and you are asking for trouble!

9. Once you have formulated your plan, stick to it! Experience shows that changing your mind repeatedly is one of the best ways to blow your budget. Your contractor will be frustrated and you'll be putting a strain on your working relationship which is likely to show in the amount of your final invoice.

10. Finally, the biggest trap of all – we call it getting personal. Don't ever carry out work that is not necessary just because you'd like to. Always remember that property developing is a business and, as such, needs to be profitable. You are not creating a home for yourself, so your particular likes and dislikes should not be part of the equation. Having thoroughly researched your market, your goal should be to satisfy the needs of that market rather than your own.

Budding Lawrence Llewellyn-Bowens will just have to keep their creative urges in check. Neutral colours and plain decoration throughout tend to get the best results.

Living the dream

After all those tough facts and figures we thought you would like to read a very heartening story about a friend of ours who has shown how property development can take you in all sorts of unexpected and lucrative directions.

Our friend Tom (not his real name – he's too modest to be identified) had been renovating older houses for about three years with moderate success. He then found a decaying building in a very desirable holiday location which he converted to three apartments. Each finished apartment was valued at around £200,000. He was about to market them all when a local estate agent pointed out to him that he could earn a substantial income from renting his apartments to holidaymakers. Tom duly investigated the possibilities and discovered to his delight that his apartments were in fact in great demand. About five minutes with a calculator confirmed to Tom that his annual income from holiday lets would allow him to borrow a further £200,000 which he has since invested in an even bigger project. The income from the apartments more than covers the interest on his borrowing.

By retaining his properties, Tom has saved a fortune in capital gains tax, estate agency and legal fees and will benefit from the growth in their value. In addition he has been able to access the capital he required for his next project without having to sell. We are all living and learning and, whilst there is an element of luck in any successful venture (as in Tom's case) it's true to say that it all starts with hard work and the satisfaction of a job well done.

I have six locks on
my door all in a row.
When I go out, I lock
every other one.
I figure no matter
how long somebody
stands there picking
the locks, they are
always locking three.

Elayne Boosler

Back to basics

chapter 8
Back to basics

In this section we are going to focus on the aspect of your development upon which everything else rests, literally – the structure of the building.

Before you even think about smart kitchens, cool bathrooms and wow factors in general you must ensure that the fabric of the building is in a good state of repair. Any structural defects will have been revealed in your survey report and therefore your renovation scheme should include correction of these defects. You should bear in mind that your buyer has a right to expect that he or she is buying a property free of problems – this is the value you are adding by carrying out the renovation.

You can rest assured that, if any significant defects are revealed in your own survey report, they will reappear when your buyer has a survey carried out. If you put yourself in the buyer's shoes for a moment, you will understand the doubt and uncertainty that arises when he or she reads the report and finds that further costly repairs are required. In short, this could kill your sale instantly!

By their very nature, they are more easily carried out at the start of any development, and thus far less expensive than having to do them at the last minute because of an adverse survey on behalf of a purchaser. Never ignore or try to camouflage structural defects.

Common problems

These are some of the most common defects that arise, particularly in older properties. They should all be included in your budget and given priority. If the problems are so serious that they cannot be rectified within budget, this will obviously have a significant impact on your potential profit, possibly even wiping it out altogether. If you are faced with such a situation the answer is simple – look for another property. Things to look out for are:

- Roof in poor condition – missing tiles or slates, rotten or damaged timbers.
- Cracks to exterior/interior walls – could indicate subsidence or 'movement'.
- Drainage in poor condition e.g. blockages or leaks in pipes.
- Rising or penetrating damp.
- Timber infestation e.g. woodworm or dry rot.
- Outdated or unsafe electrical wiring.

In all such cases, employ a professional contractor to carry out the necessary work. Not only will you be using someone who is an expert in their field, but you will also have redress if anything should go wrong. If you are employing a general building contractor, make sure that he can bring in the required expertise.

Once you have had the work done, one of the most satisfying things is to be able to show your prospective purchaser that you have taken the time, trouble and incurred the expense necessary to provide him or her with a new home that is in top condition. In our experience, reference in the estate agent's particulars to the remedial work can be regarded as a good selling point. 'Recently rewired to current regulatory standards' or 'Specialist timber treatment and damp-proofing carried out with 20-year guarantee'. Such phrases demonstrate to your potential buyer that the future will be trouble-free. This is a matter of personal choice, but on occasion we have left photocopies of rewiring certificates and timber guarantees in a prominent place in our properties so that viewers can immediately see that we haven't merely done a cosmetic makeover.

A nice touch is to put together an information pack in a plastic wallet file and leave that around for prospective purchasers when viewing. Alternatively leave a supply of paper leaflets to be taken and read later answering frequently asked questions such as;

- What new equipment has been installed and is it guaranteed?
- What remedial work has been done – is that guaranteed?
- Council tax details.
- Local information for those from another area – schools, transport, amenities etc.

All this gives the impression that you actually care about what you are selling and who you are selling it to.

Planning permission and building regulations

For the novice property developer, these phrases often spell trouble. It's true, for most of us, they can sometimes feel like a hindrance, but once you understand the reasons for their existence and the procedures involved, you will soon regard them as part of your working life. Let's see if the following helps to make sense of it all.

Planning permission

Whatever the work you plan to do, don't start before you have checked with the council's planning department as to any requirement for planning permission. There are many alterations that do not require planning permission, but you might be surprised to learn that even some minor alterations do. As a rule of thumb, it is useful to bear in mind that work usually requiring permission is that which results in a changed exterior appearance of a property, a change to its use, or work that might have an impact on neighbouring properties or the public highway.

Properties within National Parks or Conservation Areas impose additional requirements. A plan, showing dimensions, materials and finishes will be sufficient to allow your planning officer to make a decision as to whether an application will be necessary.

In the first instance, a 'phone call to a duty planning officer will be of help. Following this, many planning departments offer a weekly 'planning surgery' where you will be able to discuss your project face-to-face with a planning officer and find out what is required. The officer will also guide you through the application process and provide the appropriate application forms.

Below are some examples of work requiring planning permission:

- Any extension of property beyond permitted development rights.

- The division of a property to provide more than one self-contained home, for example flats or bed-sits.

- Division of a property for part commercial, part domestic use.

- The building of a new house in your garden.

- Any work that could obstruct a view of the highway access.

- Any work providing a parking space for a commercial vehicle.

- Work requiring new or enlarged access to a classified or major road.

Mistakes at this stage can be expensive and time-consuming so make use of all the available information from your planning department at the earliest opportunity. Help is always at hand and planning officers will generally welcome your enquiries before work starts because this makes life easier for everyone concerned.

Building regulations

This is an entirely separate matter from planning permission. Your work might not require planning permission, but depending on the nature of the work, building regulations approval could still be required. It is worth remembering that you will be committing a criminal offence if you carry out work without the necessary approval. Furthermore, when you come to sell your property you will be required by law to disclose the details of any work done and produce evidence of building regulations approval. As with planning permission, absence of such approval could result in your buyer being advised to pull out or, at best, your being forced to accept a reduced price. The following list of examples is a good indication of what you are liable to encounter:

- Removal of a load-bearing wall or any other part of the building, affecting its structure.
- Installation of any new heating appliances, e.g. a gas fire or central heating boiler. This does not apply to electrical heating appliances.
- The building of new flues or chimneys.
- Underpinning.
- Alterations for new doors and windows in roofs or walls.
- Cavity wall insulation.
- Electrical rewiring.
- Re-siting of a kitchen or bathroom.
- Extensions.
- Any new building within the grounds of your property.

- Cellar or loft conversions.
- Re-roofing, unless you are using materials identical to the originals.

You have probably gathered that the prime reason for the existence of building regulations is safety, so you will need to demonstrate to the building control department that the alterations you are carrying out will ultimately result in the property being a safe environment. Your local department will issue you with a set of guidelines and application forms on request. An officer will then visit you at the property to advise you on the exact requirements. As long as you adhere to these, there is no reason why you should not be issued with a Building Regulations Approval Certificate once the completed work has been inspected. You will need to produce this certificate to your purchaser. A fee is payable for this service, usually based on a set amount per dwelling followed by a separate charge for each inspection visit.

We have always found that telephone queries are always met with a helpful approach, though it usually makes sense to call before 10.00am or after 4.30pm – between these times a busy inspector will be out of the office, inspecting!

Always have a notebook and pen with you on site. When discussions take place with your building inspector, note carefully what is said so that there is no misunderstanding about what needs to be done.

Building inspector – friend or enemy?

It would not be fair to write about Building Regulations without introducing you to The Building Inspector, or Building Control Officer. We can only speak from experience and this particular expert has always turned out to be a reliable friend.

If you have followed the correct procedure and involved your local Building Control Department from the start, you should find that your inspector is an invaluable source of help and advice. If you are unsure about what you can and can't do, he will advise you accordingly, before it's too late. With all the new legislation flying around, our friendly inspector is something of a walking miracle. We have been constantly amazed at how he has managed to actually leave his office and inspect anything!

The volume and detail of building regulation that now exists is daunting not only in its complexity, but also in its interpretation. We have been fortunate enough to receive advice on matters such as sound insulation, fire prevention and even refuse disposal! Our inspectors have even made suggestions as to the most economical ways in which to comply with regulations, suggesting materials and methods alike.

> **DID YOU KNOW … ?**
> There is a huge amount of information available on the Internet on the subject of Building Regulations. As entertainment, it might be the perfect cure for insomnia, but just Google "Building Regulations" and you'll see what we mean. These days there is little excuse for lack of knowledge – it's all at our fingertips!

The obvious – and how not to overlook it

It's sometimes useful to look back at past mistakes and share them in the hope that you won't fall into the same trap.

So, you have decided to convert a large dilapidated Victorian terraced house into two flats. It is close to the town centre and has all mains services – gas, water and electricity. If you have ever lived in a flat, you will have taken for granted that you have your own supply of all three services – obvious. What ceased to be obvious in our case was that we had to apply to all three utility companies for a new supply for one of the flats, (the existing supplies would service the other) and that three new meters were to be fitted.

This process was extremely long-winded, not to mention costly and involved excavation of the street on three occasions, many 'phone calls and lots of form-filling! The utility companies were obliged to give notice of the intended road-works to the local authority who, on this occasion, refused on the basis that traffic and parking would be disrupted during the peak Christmas shopping period. Beware the obvious!

> **DID YOU KNOW … ?**
> When arranging a gas or water supply you are obliged to deal with 3 separate businesses – the supplier, the infrastructure engineers and the contractors who actually carry out the work on site. This means that there are 3 chances for things to go wrong, 3 lines of communication and they all have to be paid for. No wonder things get expensive and take forever. You have been warned!

> Nobody untrained in geometry may enter my house.

Plato, 428BC–348BC

Let work commence!

chapter 9
Let work commence!

When you get to this point in your project you really do need to have your wits about you. If you haven't employed a project manager (let's face it, few of us can afford to!) the key elements of the job in progress rest firmly on your shoulders – timing, budget, quality, supply of materials, provision of labour etc. The preparation of a full work schedule will be invaluable at this stage.

Here are a few basic pointers to begin with:

- Have important dates been agreed with everyone concerned?
- Have you warned the neighbours?
- Are you and your contractors complying with Health & Safety legislation?
- Are all insurances in place.
- Have you ordered all necessary materials?
- Can they be delivered on time?
- Are essential services (water, electricity) available?
- Is all your finance in place?
- Have you obtained all necessary permission to start work?
- Have you firmly agreed all quotations and prices in writing?

Keep referring back to this checklist as you prepare for work to start. There might be other reminders you wish to add relating to your specific project.

The schedule

This should ideally be in the form of a sizeable wall chart so that everyone involved can readily see what's happening. You might also like to have a smaller version, say A4, to keep with you at times when you are off site. The schedule, preferably in a calendar format, should include the following:

- Job description.
- Job cost.
- Job start and end date.
- Timing of materials deliveries.

By referring regularly to your schedule you will be able to monitor progress and, even more importantly, see where things might go wrong and take appropriate action. Also, by including the cost of each job in the schedule, you will be keeping a constant eye on your budget. Remember, don't make changes unless they are absolutely necessary, and if there are any changes proposed involving additional expense they should only be made if they will make your property more marketable.

Another useful thing you can do is to add a list of important telephone numbers to your schedule so that they are readily available in case of the inevitable emergency calls you'll have to make when people or materials don't turn up!

Finally on this subject, try to take a few quiet moments at the end of the day to check what is due to happen over the next few days. As well as avoiding problems, this will also give you a clear picture of how the job is progressing and highlight any matters needing extra attention.

Turn things around as quickly as possible. The sooner the property is finished, the sooner you can make a return on your investment.

Change your mind?

Remember, don't make changes unless they are absolutely necessary, and if any changes are proposed that involve additional expense they should only be made if they will make your property more marketable.

The list of work

Not all of the following will apply to your project, but this list should help you plan a sensible running order for the work required. No plumber is going to be amused if he arrives on time to find that you haven't taken delivery of the bathroom suite!

Common sense will tell you that the order of work might change depending on circumstances. For example, if your roof is in a particularly dilapidated state you will need to fix that before starting anything else. If your roof is not watertight, any other work could be seriously at risk.

Basic preparation:

Strip out all unwanted furniture, fixtures and fittings.

Cover all areas requiring protection from dirt, dust etc.

Demolition:

If load bearing walls are to be removed, ensure adequate support is in place.

Demolish and make sure that any plumbing or electrical wiring is disconnected and removed along with all debris.

Services:

These include drains, water supply, gas, electricity and

telephones. Any groundworks relating to these should be laid at this stage. You can then arrange for these to be connected.

Specialist treatments:

- These should always be carried out by specialist contractors. Only then will you be able to pass on guarantees to your buyer.
- Rising damp should be cured by removal of plaster to a height of one metre and injection of a chemical damp-proof course.
- Woodworm, beetle infestation and dry rot should all be treated by exposure and spraying of the affected timbers and floorboards. Any rotten timbers should be removed and replaced.
- Chimneys should be swept and flues relined.

Building:

- New or altered brickwork to be started, including insertion of doors windows, lintels etc. Don't forget to provide for piping, cabling, meters etc.
- Existing brickwork to be repaired, repointed or rerendered where required.
- Solid floors to be laid including damp-proof membrane and any insulation required.
- Fill in groundworks.
- Erect and insulate any new interior walls.
- Incorporate new timberwork and replace old as necessary.
- Replaster as required.
- New joinery where necessary.

Plumbing and water supply:

- Ensure mains supply to property.
- Run hot and cold supply to bathrooms, kitchen and outside tap.
- Install pipework and tanks for central heating system.
- Install and commission central heating boiler.
  N.B. This must be carried out by a CORGI registered installer if it is fuelled by gas.
- Install basic carcasses for kitchen and bathroom.
- Connect waste pipes in kitchen and bathroom.
- Install and connect kitchen and bathroom fittings.

Telephone, electricity and gas:

- Install pipework for all gas appliances.
- Fix (1) all electrical wiring. Do not connect to supply at this stage.
- Fix (2) light fittings, power sockets and switches. Connect to supply.
- Fit new consumer unit (fuse box) if required.

Roofing and floors:

- Repair or renew roof and supporting structure if required. Insulate.
- Fit rainwater goods, vents and soil pipes.

Initial finishing:

- Floor and wall tiling.
- Decorative joinery (skirtings, cornices, architraves etc.).

Fittings:

- All fixed units and appliances in bathroom, kitchen, shower and W.C.
- Wardrobes in bedrooms.

Final decoration:

- Filling and sanding of walls, ceilings and joinery.
- Prime and undercoat interior and exterior woodwork where necessary.
- Apply final paint/paper finishes.

Outside:

- Clear all rubbish from site.
- Landscape and plant gardens.
- Clean exterior paintwork and windows.
- Ensure that any exterior lighting is working, (particularly in winter).

As we said earlier, it's important to remember that the above list is a guide that can be tailored to your individual project. Its main purpose is to help you ensure that nothing is overlooked.

Unless you are gifted with a superhuman memory, lists are by far the best way of ensuring that everything that needs to be done IS done. However they become pointless and irritating if you don't take the trouble to work through them diligently. Trust us, a list of 10 items with 10 ticks is a thing of beauty – only 5 ticks and it becomes a beast!

"I've never lived
in a building without
my name on it.

Ivana Trump

Managing
the job

chapter 10
Managing the job

Are you up to it? It's certainly not the easiest of jobs but if you are considering running the whole project yourself, you really need to find out if you are the kind of person who can handle it. Answer the following questions – and be honest with the answers!

- Am I good at dealing with people?
- Am I disciplined?
- Do I like to work methodically & efficiently?
- Do I have a head for figures?
- Am I able to devote some time each day to being on site?
- Am I happy with the prospect of some hard work?
- Can I absorb and retain information easily and am I willing to learn?
- Am I patient?
- Can I remain calm under stress?
- Am I able to have 'difficult' conversations? (i.e. could I fire someone or tell them that their service is not good enough?)
- Am I persistent and resourceful when the going gets tough?

If you can answer "yes" to all the above, you'll make an excellent project manager and you're probably superhuman too! (or at least you think you are). To explain exactly what's involved, the following tips should help you on your way.

Project managing

- Have your tradesmen lined up by the time contracts are exchanged. That goes for materials too. By that time you will have a firm date for completion so you will know when work can start.

- Have a contingency list of back-up tradesmen and suppliers at the ready in case you are let down at the last minute. Personal recommendation is always a good source. This is also a great way to build up useful contacts for the future.

- Draw up your chart (see Chapter 9) based on the work schedule. This should be displayed on site so that everyone knows what's happening, and when. It's important to make sure that materials arrive on time, though you don't want the site cluttered with items that won't be needed for a while. Too much 'stuff' around makes working difficult and there's also a risk of accidental damage.

- Always ensure that you have written agreements with your tradesmen as to the nature and extent of work required and, of course, the cost. Only then are you in a position to control your budget properly. If extra or unforeseen work is required, again make sure this is the subject of an additional agreement. This rule applies to sub-contractors too. Time and time again we have seen problems arising from failure to make everything absolutely clear from the outset. The result is usually unpleasant and costly.

- As project manager, you need to be in control at all times. This means actually being on site as often as possible. You need to check the progress and quality of work so that you are able to pay on time, and your tradesman will need regular contact with you to discuss any unforeseen problems or changes. For the time when you can't be on site, it's a good idea to display your mobile 'phone number on the chart so that it's readily available if a member of your team needs to get in touch urgently.

- Never take on too much. Some renovation projects can be very complex, so if you feel that you might be out of your depth don't hesitate to ask for expert help – in the long run it will save you hassle and money.

- Paperwork is important, so keep on top of it. Think of it as your 'road map to success'. It might seem like a lot of annoying bits of paper, but a tidy, well organised file for your project will save you time, money and a good deal of anxiety. Much of the paperwork is vital if your eventual sale is to go through without a hitch. Items such as guarantees and certificates for specialist work should be kept safe for passing on to your purchaser. If you don't feel that confident about office management it's a good idea to hand over such documents to your solicitor in readiness for completion.

- If you are busy enough to have two or more projects ongoing at the same time, the same tips will apply to each. However, there will be a degree of extra 'juggling' involved if you are to keep things running smoothly. The tips that follow should help you achieve that all-important balance.

- Don't take on too much financially. If you jeopardize your cash flow situation you'll be heading for trouble.

- As usual, don't avoid asking for help, particularly where site management is concerned – no one can be in two places at once!

- You'll be keeping an eye on two or more budgets, so keep your paperwork tidy so that you always have a clear picture of your spending.

- Under no circumstances should your budgets merge. In other words, don't subsidise overspending on one budget by 'borrowing' from another. This borrowing will never be paid back and you will be left with a financial mess. Each project needs to be viable in its own right in accordance with your original plan and budget.

- Looking on the bright side, if you're buying twice as much plasterboard, two bathroom suites or two complete kitchens you'll be able to negotiate better deals on prices with your suppliers, so adding more to your bottom line.

- Finally, don't panic. If there's a problem, take some time to think carefully about a solution, taking advice if necessary. In developing, hasty decisions are usually costly.

Health and safety

You can't possibly be expected to know in detail about all the regulations that exist in this very important aspect of development, but, as ever, you will need to be aware of those that apply to your activities. For this reason, we suggest that you either:

1. Contact the Health & Safety Executive Information Line on 08701 545500 with any queries.

2. Visit their website from which you can download useful free leaflets on the subject. **www.hse.gov.uk.**

Buying materials

This is a matter for you; there is nothing written in stone as to who does what. The important thing is that you get what you need, when you need it, at the best price.

Always ask your contractor/builder to provide costings for materials within his quotation. In our experience it is often possible to obtain better prices than our builder. Some builders positively welcome your taking the responsibility for this aspect, leaving them to simply get on with the job.

If you are relatively inexperienced, you will need to make sure that your order is correctly specified – ask your builder/contractor to make you a 'shopping list'. Timing is the other vital factor. Any savings you make on price could disappear if materials aren't delivered on time – and then that's your responsibility.

Here are some useful pointers on suppliers and supplies:

DIY retailers

Though not quite as keen on price as builders' merchants for core building materials, they do stock many items besides that you might not always find at your local merchants, such as light fittings, electrical goods, hand and power tools etc. They can also be great in an emergency because of their seven-day opening hours, often until 8.00 or 10.00 p.m. during the week and until 4.00 or 5.00 p.m. on Sundays. If you run out of paint or break your last jigsaw blade on a Sunday morning, help is at hand!

Don't get carried away
– decide on how much
you want to spend
and then stick to it.
How many property
programmes have you
seen where they go
wildly over budget?
Well – learn from it!

Builders' merchants

For most basic building materials, this will be your first port of call. They can supply the majority of your requirements, but don't expect a huge choice when it comes to decorative or finishing materials. If you decide to set yourself up as a business, consider opening a trade account which will give you a monthly credit facility. This will make paperwork easier to manage and assist your cash flow.

Go and introduce yourself and your business to the manager, tell him what you're looking for and open a trade account. Don't ever be afraid to negotiate on price. It's likely that you will start with a particular level of discount that will increase over time as your spending increases. Needless to say, as in all your business dealings, make sure you pay on time. You will be taken seriously and, as a reliable customer you will be entitled to a reliable service and competitive prices.

Hardware shops

Often seen as a last resort, hardware shops can be incredibly useful for those items that the big retailers just don't stock. They also tend to stock items that you can buy in small quantities or even individually. A single tap washer will cost you less than a pack of three from your local large DIY retailer.

Plumbers' merchants

Here you can buy everything you need for bathrooms and central heating systems, usually at the most competitive prices. As with all trade suppliers, open an account and negotiate your trade discount.

Ready-mixed concrete

As long as access is not a problem, this is by far the best way to buy concrete to cover a large area. Not only is it time and labour saving, but it's also cheaper than mixing it on site. Sold by the cubic metre, the price will vary depending on your location in relation to the depot and the type of mix required.

Glass

As a general rule, small local firms will supply you for single glazing and repair jobs. For double glazing you will need to use a specialist manufacturer/supplier of which, fortunately, there is no shortage. When replacing windows and doors, bear in mind Building Regulations in force since 2002. The glazing must conform to certain standards relating to energy conservation and safety on impact.

Crushed stone

This is ideal for hardcore beneath foundations or concrete slab. It's relatively cheap, though the price you pay will again depend on the distance involved in the delivery.

Sand and aggregate

Simply buy in bulk from your local quarry company – it's cheaper.

What does a project manager do all day?

Even if you decide not to undertake this task yourself, you should still have a clear idea of what the job involves, if only to ensure that your chosen manager is on top of things. Here are the important aspects of the job:

1. Hiring all tradesmen and subcontractors.
2. Preparing a schedule of works and making sure that work is done in accordance with the schedule, both on time and within budget.
3. Responsibility for safety on site.
4. Responsibility for meeting legal requirements, e.g. Party Wall Agreements, parking etc.
5. Ordering all materials and ensuring that they arrive in the right place at the right time in perfect condition.
6. Making all major decisions.
7. Ensuring that the site is tidy and all debris is cleared away.
8. Ensuring that workers have tea and coffee available, along with toilet facilities.
9. Being on site at least once a day and assisting with labour if the job falls behind schedule.
10. Total responsibility for the smooth running of the site throughout the project.

The building contract

If you decide that running the project yourself is either impractical or just not for you, then you really need to employ a contractor or project manager to do the job for you. It's therefore wise to have a contract in place for the entire job. If you want to know what to include, the list below should be of some help. To make the exercise even easier you could try downloading a ready-made form of contract published by the Federation of Master Builders and available free of charge on their website (**www.fmb.org.uk**). All you will need to do is complete it with the details appropriate to your project. Your contractor does not have to be an F.M.B. member to use this document.

These are some of the main aspects covered by such a contract:

- A detailed schedule of all works required.

- A series of clauses describing the contractor's responsibilities. With materials you would be wise to specify 'all materials included, with the exception of................'.

- Insurance, including public and employers' liability. Ideally you should see evidence of these before work commences.

- Quality of work; the use of skilled labour; work to be done in accordance with accepted good practice; fixing and handling of materials in accordance with manufacturers' instructions; mistakes and sub-standard work to be rectified at the contractor's expense.

- Contractor to ensure that all materials and structures are adequately protected at all times.

- Contractor to take all reasonable precautions with regard to waste disposal and nuisance to neighbours and the general public, including supervision of deliveries and obstruction of roads.
- All necessary tools, equipment and scaffolding to be provided by the contractor.
- Parties to agree on the provision of essential services (water, gas, electricity).
- Contractor to be responsible for ensuring that all works comply with planning permission, Party Wall Agreements and Building Regulations and for obtaining the necessary certificates.
- Any contract entered into with sub-contractors to embody the same terms as those specified in the main contract.
- No variations to the contract terms without prior agreement between the parties.

Not only will such a contract offer you protection, but it will also act as a checklist for reference during the life of the project, helping things run smoothly for everyone involved.

Our first couple of projects did not involve written contracts of any description. Whilst we didn't suffer any great loss or disadvantage as a result, there were several occasions when we wished we had been more insistent on written contracts. Misunderstandings, disagreements and sub-standard workmanship are far more easily handled when there is a contract in existence.

It's really the cat's house – we just pay the mortgage.

Anon

Buy to let

chapter 11
Buy to let

So far we have been concentrating on buying, renovating and selling. However, many of you will have thought about the prospect of buying property, renovating where necessary and then letting. This can be a great way of initially creating a second income or building some security for the future.

At the time of writing, with interest rates rising steadily, it's becoming increasingly difficult to create a meaningful income from buy to let. For most investors, buying to let means there's a mortgage that has to be paid. This means that the higher the interest rate, the greater your mortgage payment and the lesser the profit. However, if you make no profit at all, you still have capital growth as the value of your property increases in the medium to long term. In the meantime, as long as your mortgage payments are wholly met by rent received, the exercise is costing you nothing. So, as interest rates rise it is obviously sensible to try to secure a fixed rate mortgage which will offer some protection against further increases.

If you enjoy the 'cut and thrust' of buying, renovating AND selling on a regular and frequent basis, you might find buy to let a little dull. But there is something to be said for doing both to provide income and capital growth. There is also the prospect of re-mortgaging your rental properties periodically to finance further projects.

The money

Getting started is nowhere near as complicated as it used to be. Almost all mortgage lenders have come to appreciate that buy to let is here to stay and is a great source of business, particularly when, because of the commercial and very slightly riskier nature of this type of lending, they are able to charge their borrowers higher rates of interest (typically 0.5% to 1.00% over the basic variable rate). As usual, shop around for the best deal, using the Internet, the press, specialist publications or, probably best of all, an Independent Financial Adviser.

Not always many happy returns

Just because you might have lived in rented accommodation does not mean you have fully understood what being a landlord is all about e.g. they tend to be there when the rent is due but not when things needs fixing. But the stereotypical image of rent books and rising damp is now being replaced by rising numbers of entrepreneurs who see buy to let as a great money-making opportunity.

It's clear that buy to let, like stepping out on any new career, still requires a thorough examination of your personal finances. Rental income needs to outstrip mortgage interest payments by between 25 and 50 per cent because if there is a gap in the rental period you will have to stump up yourself. Could you afford to pay both the loan on an investment property and the mortgage on your own house if you had no rent coming in? While buy to let is clearly a viable business opportunity don't rush into a rental property and end up overstretching your finances, because the returns might not be as much as you think.

Buy a property that is suitable for both resell and rental, so as to maximise your opportunity for profit. As one market declines the other will often pick up.

The figures

In most cases your maximum loan will be 85% of the current market value. However, the lender will also stipulate that the anticipated rental value must be able to cover the monthly mortgage interest by at least 115%. This is a safety net for both you and the lender to provide for occasional 'voids' – when the property is empty and no rent is being received, and tenants who might fall into arrears. If all this is as clear as mud, don't worry – here's an example:

Value of Property – £120,000.

Maximum mortgage – 85% – £102,000. Deposit required = £18,000.

Monthly interest payable at 6.50% p.a. = £552.50.

Minimum monthly rent required = £552.50 x 115% = £635.37.

In this case, if you were able to raise £18,000 deposit and knew from your research that you could achieve a rental income of say £650 per month, then this deal would work for you.

Looking at the bigger picture, you might have heard the term "yield" mentioned in commercial property circles. As a potential landlord, this is something you need to understand. 'Yield' means the annual rental income generated by a property expressed as a percentage of its value.

So, in the example above, if we assume that it yields a rental income of £650 per month, this means an annual income of £7,800. Expressed as a percentage of the property value, (£120,000), we can say that the 'yield' in relation to this property is 6.50%, (£7,800 being 6.50% of £120,000).

As a rule, you shouldn't be seriously looking at any property with a yield of less than 5.00%. Obviously, rents can fall as well as rise depending on market conditions, and even though interest rates are currently very low, they can rise dramatically too. Taking these matters into account, along with the continuing costs of letting, such as maintenance, management fees and insurance, there needs to be adequate room for manoeuvre should the going get tough.

Building a portfolio

If you manage to buy well and renovate, it's likely that the value of your property will have already increased prior to letting. This, coupled with the passage of time in a rising market could put you in a position where you are able to borrow further funds in order to finance the purchase of another property. This process is called 'building a portfolio'. Let's say you bought your property a year ago for £120,000 with a mortgage of £102,000, carried out some improvement work, and were then able to achieve a rental income of £575 per month. An up-to-date valuation reveals that the property is now worth £150,000. Using the example above, you would now be able to increase your borrowing from £102,000 to £120,000, leaving you with £18,000 to invest in your next buy to let property.

We know that this sounds easy, but we can't over-emphasise the need to be as thorough and as careful as possible in your planning and research. Being left with a number of properties on your hands with little or no income to support your borrowing is nothing short of financial disaster. Always run your proposals by your financial adviser to get an objective view.

The finish

When carrying out your renovation, you must still bear in mind your market. With lettings, your market is substantially different. You must acknowledge that the average tenant will not look after your property in the same way as you or any other owner would. For this reason, kitchens, bathrooms, carpets, floor coverings, curtains/blinds and other fixtures and fittings should be serviceable, hard-wearing but not expensive. All are likely to take more than their fair share of knocks during a tenancy, and you are the one who will have the expense of repair and replacement.

The garden

Generally speaking, you should aim to make your rental property a low maintenance proposition, both inside and out. This is particularly true of the garden. Large gardens are usually a disaster, simply because the average tenant is essentially requiring a temporary home and will have neither the interest nor the commitment to look after a garden properly. So, if your property has a garden, design it with a non-gardener in mind. You can use shingle, pebbles, a patio and perhaps two or three pots or planters containing shrubs to 'soften' the area and provide colour. If you feel that there simply must be a lawn, don't go for anything too extensive – your tenants won't thank you for it, and you could end up with a jungle when they depart! One point you might like to consider; if the lawn is neat and tidy when your tenants arrive and you provide them with a mower, you have a much greater chance of avoiding the 'jungle' effect when they leave.

Décor

The same will apply with décor. Neutral colours and a good professional finish will suffice – don't go overboard with expensive paint, fabrics or other materials.

Furniture and appliances

Turning again to indoor matters, the question of furnishing arises. To furnish, or not to furnish – that's the question. There is no hard and fast rule here, it's really a matter of common sense. For example, if you are likely to be letting to students, then it's sensible to assume that they will not have furniture of their own. In our experience, when letting to professionals and families, furniture is certainly not a requirement and in fact could be a disadvantage. Many people prefer to have their own 'stuff' around them – it's a way of making someone else's property feel more like home.

It is worth bearing in mind though, that in a competitive market, the provision of good working appliances such as cookers, washing machines, fridges, freezers and dishwashers will all help your property to stand out amongst the rest and enable you to achieve maximum rental income. A vacuum cleaner also provides an incentive for your tenant to at least keep the place clean. You should remember that it is your responsibility to ensure that all these items are safe by having them regularly tested and, of course, they must be kept in full working order if they are provided as part of the tenancy agreement.

Insurance

It will certainly be a condition of your mortgage that the property is insured at all times, but it is also your legal obligation as a landlord to do so. Don't forget to include this cost in your overall calculations as to viability.

Taxation

Since rent received is income, you are therefore liable to payment of income tax and must declare the appropriate amounts on your tax return. You will receive allowances in respect of your legitimate costs such as insurance, maintenance and agents' fees, etc. The services of an accountant can be invaluable here – you're entitled to claim allowances for those too!

Managing your rental property

If you decide not to part with 15% of your rental income each month to pay for the services of a letting agent, you need to know what you have to do in order to maximise that benefit, but be warned, it does involve a high degree of organisation, as well as a substantial amount of work on your part!

- Never let to friends, relatives or business colleagues – you're asking for trouble.

- Have an Assured Shorthold Tenancy Agreement drawn up, either by your solicitor or by using a ready-made form which is widely available. It's a legally binding document specifically designed to protect you, your tenant and your mortgage lender (who will usually insist on it).

- Keep a handy list of tradesmen whom you can contact in the event of an emergency or urgent repair being required. Trying to find a 24-hour plumber in Yellow Pages at 3.00 a.m. is neither fun nor cost-effective!

- Always obtain contact details from your tenant and be sure to provide your own telephone number etc. – you should be able to contact each other at all times in case of emergency.

- Make your tenants aware that you will be calling to inspect the property at regular intervals, e.g. quarterly, and agree that you will give them seven days' notice of your visit. This is an opportunity for them to highlight any concerns or mention any maintenance requirements. It's also a chance for you to make sure that they aren't keeping baby alligators in the bath!

- Always keep at least two spare sets of keys available for tradesmen or your tenants if they should lose them.

- Provide instructions for the use of appliances and have the central heating boiler serviced regularly.

- Take meter readings at the start and end of each tenancy, preferably in the presence of your tenants. This will avoid any possible disputes over unpaid utility bills.

- Insist that rent is paid monthly by standing order to avoid costly and messy collection of rent.

No man acquires property without acquiring with it a little arithmetic also.

Ralph Waldo Emerson

Checklists, conversion charts & contacts

External works – checklist & budget

	Work required	Cost
EXTERNAL:		
Demolition		
Site clearance		
Roof		
Chimney		
Windows/doors		
Guttering		
Brickwork		
New building		
Extension		
Painting		
Skip hire		
Utilities		
Aerials		
Labour costs		

	Work required	Cost
GARDEN:		
Hard landscaping		
Planting		
Water feature		
Labour costs		
STRUCTURES:		
Shed		
Garage		
Labour costs		
EQUIPMENT & TOOLS:		
Hire		
Purchase		
Consumables		
Total materials:		
Total labour:		
VAT:		
TOTAL COST OF WORK:		

Internal works – checklist & budget

To create an accurate schedule and checklist, we recommend that you go through the property systematically and, room by room, detail the work that is required and divide it into the following categories.

This will give you a clear picture of the amount of work you are taking on, whilst providing you with an instant guide to the various skills you will need to bring in to complete the project.

Again, no generic list can be exhaustive, so there might well be other matters you would wish to include relating to your particular project. Even if specifics aren't included here, the list will certainly provide a good place to start and help you to start planning. Once you have a complete list of all the internal works required you can draw up a checklist and budget similar to the one for the external works on the previous page.

Major works – new walls, floors, extensions etc.

Kitchen – units, sinks, taps.

Bathroom – suite, shower, wastes.

Joinery – doors, skirtings, storage, shelves etc.

Plumbing – central heating, kitchen, bathroom etc.

Windows – repair and replacement, additions etc.

Tiling – kitchen, bathroom, flooring, fireplaces etc.

Electrics – rewiring, new sockets, switches, phones etc.

Decoration – woodwork, walls and ceilings.

Walls and ceilings – plaster repair and replastering.

Flooring – laying screeds, concrete, wood and vinyl, carpeting.

Example of a simple building contract

Builder's Name ....

Address ....

....

....

Client's Name ....

Address ....

....

....

Schedule of Work

....

....

....

....

....

....

....

Start Date ....

Finish Date ....

Total Price ....

VAT at .... %

Signatures

.... The Builder

.... The Client

Date ....

Wallpaper calculator

Distance around room		Height of room		
(m)	(ft)	2.15–2.30m (7–7.5ft)	2.30–2.45m (7.5–8ft)	2.45–2.60m (8–8.5ft)
9 m	29.5 ft	4	5	5
10 m	33 ft	5	5	5
12 m	39.5 ft	5	6	6
13 m	42.5 ft	6	6	7
14 m	46 ft	6	7	7
15 m	49 ft	7	7	8
16 m	52.5 ft	7	8	9
17 m	56 ft	8	8	9
19 m	62.5 ft	8	9	10
20 m	65.5 ft	9	9	10
21 m	69 ft	9	10	11
22 m	72 ft	10	10	12
24 m	77 ft	10	11	12
25 m	82 ft	11	11	13
26 m	85.5 ft	12	12	14
27 m	88.5 ft	12	13	14
29 m	95 ft	13	13	15
30 m	98.5 ft	13	14	15

When choosing wallpaper always check the batch/shade numbers are the same. Make sure you buy enough wallpaper to finish the job. Any unopened rolls can be returned for a refund. This chart is for guidance only. For large patterned wallpaper you will need to allow extra rolls for matching.

The distance around the room includes windows and radiators and the wall height is from skirting board.

Tile calculator

Tile size		Quantity required	
Metric (mm)	Imperial (in)	per sq. metre	per sq. yard
100x100	4″ x 4″	100	84
108x108	4.25″ x 4.25″	86	72
150x150	6″ x 6″	44	36
200x100	8″ x 4″	50	41
200x150	8″ x 6″	33	27
200x200	8″ x 8″	25	20
225x150	9″ x 6″	29	24
225x225	9″ x 9″	20	16
250x150	10″ x 6″	27	22
250 x150	10″ x 10″	16	13
250x250	12″ x 8″	17	14
300x200	12″ x 12″	11	9
300x300	13″ x 13″	9	8

This chart might help you when buying tiles. Remember to buy some extra just in case you suffer breakages.

Conversion charts

WEIGHT & MEASURE CONVERSIONS

Length:		
1 millimetre (mm)		= 0.0394 inch (in)
1 centimetre (cm)	= 10 mm	= 0.0394 in
1 metre (m)	= 100 cm	= 1.0936 yard (yd)
1 kilometre (km)	= 1,000 m	= 0.6214 mile

1 inch		= 2.54 cm
1 foot (ft)	= 12 in	= 0.3048 m
1 yard	= 3 ft	= 0.9144 m
1 mile	= 1,760 yd	= 1.6093 km

Area:		
1 square cm (cm^2)	= 100 mm^2	= 0.1550 in^2
1 square m (m^2)	= 10,000 cm^2	= 1.1960 yd^2
1 square km (km^2)	= 100 hectares	= 0.3861 mile^2

1 square in (in^2)		= 6.4516 cm^2
1 square ft (ft^2)	= 144 in^2	= 0.0929 m^2
1 square yd (yd^2)	= 9 ft^2	= 0.8361 m^2
1 acre	= 4,840 yd^2	= 4,046.9 m^2
1 square mile	= 640 acres	= 2.590 km^2

Volume:		
1 cubic cm (cm³)		= 0.0610 in³
1 cubic decimetre (dm³)	= 1,000 cm³	= 0.0353 ft³
1 cubic m (m³)	= 1,000 dm³	= 1.3080 yd³
1 litre (l)	= 1 dm³ = 1000 millilitre = 2.113 US pt	= 1.76 pint (pt)
1 hectolitre (hl)	= 100 l	= 21.997 gallon = 26.417 US gallon

1 cubic in (in³)		= 16.387 cm³
1 cubic ft (ft³)	= 1,728 in³	= 0.0283 m³
1 cubic yd (yd³)	= 27 ft³	= 0.7646 m³
1 fluid ounce (fl oz)		= 28.413 ml
1 pint (pt)	= 20 fl oz	= 0.5683 l
1 gallon (gal)	= 8 pt	= 4.546 l = 1.201 US gallon

Mass:		
1 milligram (mg)		= 0.0154 grain
1 gram (g)	= 1,000 mg	= 0.0353 ounce (oz)
1 metric carat	= 0.2 g	= 3.0865 grains
1 kilogram (kg)	= 1,000 g	= 2.2046 pound (lb)
1 tonne (t)	= 1,000 kg	= 0.9842 ton

1 oz	= 437.5 grains	= 28.35 g
1 lb	= 16 oz	= 0.4536 kg
1 stone	= 14 lb	= 6.3503 kg
1 hundredweight (cwt)	= 112 lb	= 50.802 kg
1 ton	= 20 cwt	= 1.016 t

Useful contacts

As you progress in property development your list of contacts is sure to grow. If you're just starting out, this list will help you on your way:

Legal and financial
Council of Mortgage Lenders
www.cml.co.uk

Her Majesty's Land Registry
www.landreg.gov.uk
020 7917 8888

Independent Financial Advisors Promotion
www.ifap.org.uk
0800 085 3250

Inland Revenue
www.inlandrevenue.gov.uk
0845 605 5999

Irish Law Society
www.lawsociety.ie
00 353 1671 0711

The Leasehold Advisory Service
www.lease-advice.org.uk
0845 345 1993

Scottish Law Information
www.scottishlaw.org.uk

Scottish Law Society
www.law.scot.org.uk
0131 226 7411

The Law Society
www.lawsociety.org.uk
0207 242 1222

The Society of Financial Advisors
www.sofa.org.uk
0208 989 8464

Trading Standards Office
www.tradingstandards.gov.uk

General research

Centre for Economics – Business Research
www.cebr.com
0207 324 2850

Department of Trade & Industry
www.dti.gov.uk
0207 215 5000

Design Council
www.design-council.org.uk/design
0207 420 5200

DfES School & College Performance Tables
www.dfes.gov.uk/performancetables
0845 933 3111

English Heritage
www.english-heritage.org.uk
0870 333 1181

Environment Agency
www.environment-agency.gov.uk
0845 933 3111

 Contacts

Homecheck: Property advice
www.homecheck.co.uk

Homesale: Network property website
www.home-sale.co.uk

Hometrack: Prices & market trends
www.hometrack.co.uk

Micropal: Standard & Poors Investment Information
www.funds-sp.com

National Approved Letting Scheme
www.nalscheme.co.uk
01242 581712

National Association of Estate Agents
www.naea.co.uk
01926 496800

National House Building Council
www.nhbc.co.uk
01494 735363

National Land Information Services
www.nlis.org.uk
01279 451625

National Rail Enquiries
www.nationalrail.co.uk
08457 484950

Office for Standards in Education
www.ofsted.gov.uk
0207 421 6800

Office of the Deputy Prime Minister
www.housing.odpm.gov.uk
0207 944 4400

Online Estate Agents
www.findaproperty.com

Rightmove: Property advice
www.rightmove.co.uk

Royal Institute of Chartered Surveyors
www.nrics.org.uk

The Historic Buildings Bureau for Scotland
www.historic-scotland.gov.uk
0131 668 8668

The Victorian Society
www.victorian-society.org.uk
0208 994 1019

Up My Street: Local information
www.upmystreet.com

Association of Residential Letting Agents
www.arla.co.uk
0845 345 5752

The building trade

Council for Registered Gas Installers (CORGI)
www.corgi-gas.com
01256 372200

Electrical Contractors Association Ltd.
www.eca.co.uk
0207 313 4800

Federation of Master Builders
www.fmb.org.uk
0207 242 7583

Gas Consumers Council
www.energywatch.org.uk
0207 931 0977

Institute of Plumbing
www.plumbers.org.uk
01708 472791

National Association of Plumbing, Heating & Mechanical Services
www.aphc.co.uk
0800 542 6060

National Federation of Roofing Contractors
www.nfrc.co.uk
0207 435 0387

Painting & Decorating Federation
0207 608 5093

The Heating & Ventilation Contractors' Association
www.hvca.org.uk
0207 313 4900

Index

'The Greatest Tips in the World' books

Pet Recipe books

The Greatest Feline Feasts in the World by Joe Inglis
ISBN 978-1-905151-50-9

The Greatest Doggie Dinners in the World by Joe Inglis
ISBN 978-1-905151-51-6

'The Greatest in the World' DVDs

The Greatest in the World – Gardening Tips
presented by Steve Brookes

The Greatest in the World – Yoga Tips
presented by David Gellineau and David Robson

The Greatest in the World – Cat & Kitten Tips
presented by Joe Inglis

The Greatest in the World – Dog & Puppy Tips
presented by Joe Inglis

For more information about currently available
and forthcoming book and DVD titles please visit:

www.thegreatestintheworld.com

or write to:

The Greatest in the World Ltd
PO Box 3182
Stratford-upon-Avon
Warwickshire CV37 7XW
United Kingdom

Tel / Fax: +44(0)1789 299616
Email: info@thegreatestintheworld.com

The authors

Brought together in 1997 by their love of writing and performing music, Fiona and Paul quickly discovered something else they had in common – a fascination with bricks and mortar. It wasn't too long before they started looking at property as more than somewhere to live. Since buying and renovating their first tiny terraced house they have become full-time developers. Every project is different so the interest and enthusiasm continues! Fiona and Paul married in 2003 and live in rural Warwickshire with their children Charlotte and Joss. They still find time for the music, but perhaps that's another book … !